A JOURNAL OF ORTHODOX FAITH AND CULTURE

ROAD TO EMMAUS
– No. 1 –

Sometimes God sends me moment
in which I am utterly at peace.
In those moments I have constructed
for myself a creed in which everything
is clear and holy for me. Here it is:
to believe that there is nothing more
beautiful, more profound, more sympathetic,
more reasonable, more courageous,
and more perfect than Christ: and not only
is there nothing, but I tell myself with
jealous love that never could there be.

FYODOR DOSTOEVSKY

International Editor: Mother Nectaria McLees
US Editor: Todd Richard Betts
Russian Co-Editor: Inna Belov
Staff Correspondents: Nicholas Karellos (Greece), Thomas Hulbert (Western Europe)
Production Manager: Bruce Petersen
Subscriptions and Shipping: Elisabeth Litster
Art Direction and Layout: Bruce Petersen
Public Relations: Stephen Litster
International Liaison: Catherine McCaffery

SUBSCRIPTIONS AND CORRESPONDENCE
Road to Emmaus, P.O. Box 16021, Portland, OR 97292-0021

Call toll-free (USA): 1-866-783-6628
Monday-Friday 9:00 am to 5:00 pm (Pacific Standard Time, USA)
Email: emmausjournal@juno.com
Web: www.roadtoemmaus.net

Published Quarterly
$30/year, $55/ 2 year, single issue $11.95. (US check or money order or by credit card on our website)

INTERNATIONAL SUBSCRIPTIONS
Canada add $10/year for shipping. Outside North America add $20/year shipping.
Please subscribe by credit card on our website: www.roadtoemmaus.net
or write us at emmausjournal@juno.com

EDITORIAL OFFICES
Valaam Society of America Russian Mission, #10 Bolshaya Pereyaslavskaya, kv. 124, Moscow, Russia 129110

PUBLISHER
Road to Emmaus Foundation, PO Box 198, Maysville, MO 64469

This periodical is indexed in the *ATLA Religion Database*, a product of the
American Theological Library Association, 300 S. Wacker Dr., Suite 2100, Chicago, IL 60606
Email: atla@atla.com   Web: www.atla.com

ISBN: 978-1-63551-001-0

A JOURNAL OF ORTHODOX FAITH AND CULTURE

ROAD TO EMMAUS

Vol. I, No. 1   Spring 2000 (#1)

―――――――――――――――― + CONTENTS + ――――――――――――――――

3   FIRE FROM HEAVEN: HOLY SATURDAY AT THE LORD'S TOMB
by Mother Nectaria McLees
Historical and contemporary accounts of the annual miracle of
the Holy Fire, which has appeared for centuries on Orthodox Holy
Saturday at the Lord's tomb in Jerusalem.

25 TEACHING OUR CHILDREN TO PRAY: REFLECTIONS OF A
YOUNG MOTHER
An interview with Moscow resident Inna Belov on her young son's
first years as a Christian.

45 FROM AMERICA TO RUSSIA: THE MYRRH-STREAMING ICON OF TSAR
NICHOLAS II
by Richard Betts
A unique record of how this icon print of Tsar Nicholas II was taken
from America to Russia and the impact and inspiration generated
by its presence in post-Soviet society.

61 SAINTS ALIVE: SURVIVORS OF A MISERABLE WRECK
In their own words, Sts. Basil the Great and Gregory the
Theologian's first humorous and disastrous attempts to live
an ascetic life in the wilderness near Cappadocia.

63 TALKS WITH ORTHODOX CHRISTIANS: MY ROAD TO EMMAUS
Five Russian Orthodox Christians describe their awakening to Christ
and his Church.

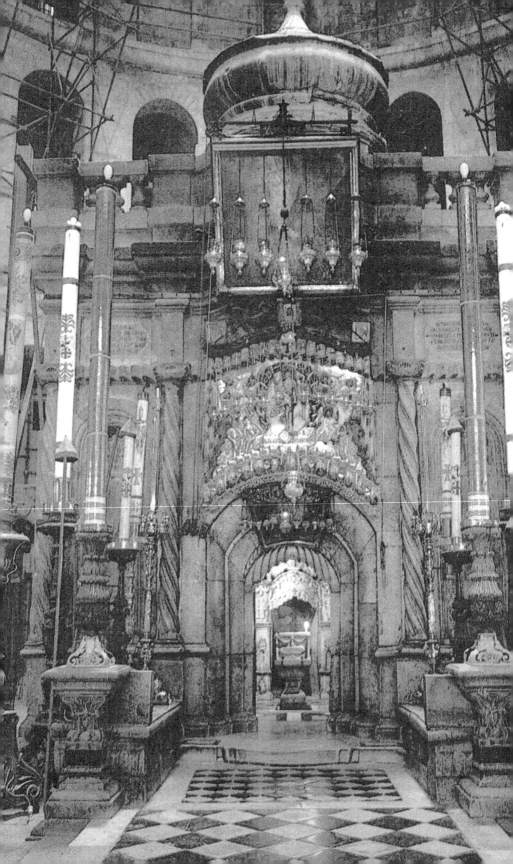

FIRE FROM HEAVEN

Holy Saturday at the Lord's Tomb

by Mother Nectaria McLees

"Do you see anything?" The question has been echoing around us for hours in Arabic, English, Russian, Albanian, Amharic, Romanian, Greek, Bulgarian...and the answer is always the same, "Not yet. Lord have mercy!" Irina and I have been in the church of the Holy Sepulchre for twenty-seven hours, hunched over tiny canvas campstools, with dried bread, fruit and a little water in bags under our feet. Since yesterday's service of the Royal Hours we have waited, alternately praying, dozing and watching our space shrink to the diameter of the stools on which we sit.... On Good Friday the funeral service of the Lord begins, and we watch as the epitaphion, the burial shroud with the embroidered image of Christ, is carried out. We are shaken. In this holy place it is as if we are watching a real funeral, and many of the pilgrims weep aloud. During the night, an old Greek woman tells us of having been thirty times to Jerusalem for Pascha. The Romanians in front of us push back further and further, trying to stretch their legs, until one of the men is sitting on my feet. He ignores my pleas to get up, and when I try to push him off, he jumps up and shakes his fist at us, shouting that we are dirty Russian Communists. I tell him loudly that we are not Communists, we are Orthodox Christians, and he subsides into angry muttering. At dawn on Saturday morning Greek latecomers, jealous of our ten-inch stools, accuse us of hoarding space. An imposing Arab man who has been here from the night before steps in as our guardian and hovers over us protectively until the Israeli police arrive at 8:30 and order everyone to their feet, pushing us together to make an aisle around the center of the church. For the next six hours we stand in a crowd packed so tightly that we have to wrench our arms up to

Opposite: The Edicule: The tomb of Christ inside the Holy Sepulchre Church, Jerusalem.

make the sign of the cross. The breaths of those around us wave against our cheeks and the back of our necks. The suffocating heat reminds us of our empty water bottles. We remind ourselves that it is fitting to suffer from thirst while the Lord is still in the tomb, and we pray God to give us pure hearts and a little more strength, that we might see the Holy Fire...

– N. Tikhonova

Although this scene took place in 1997, it is a Paschal vigil familiar to Orthodox Christian pilgrims for centuries: the timelessness of Holy Week services and the long wait before the descent of the grace-filled fire on Holy Saturday. Few English-speaking Christians outside the Orthodox Church know of the Holy Fire, and those who do often believe it to be a hoax. Orthodox converts in the West may not even hear of it until they celebrate their first Pascha, when it descends with the shock of ice water over carefully reasoned conversions. "Do you mean that fire actually comes down from heaven to the Lord's Tomb in Jerusalem on Holy Saturday, and everyone sees it?" That is precisely what is meant. And what the Orthodox have claimed for centuries.

We Orthodox Christians are like children. Although we have eagerly watched the Holy Fire descend for centuries, we know nothing about how it comes or even when it first began. It is universally accepted in Eastern Christendom as a heavenly manifestation, yet surviving accounts of the Fire's miraculous character date only from the ninth century.

Earlier sources, among them a fourth-century diary of the Spanish nun-pilgrim Egeria and later lectionaries from Armenia, Georgia, and St. Sabbas Monastery, detail the Paschal services, including a candle lighting ritual cel- ebrating Christ's resurrection. The ritual was part of Holy Saturday vespers, the origin of the "new light" by which the church was illuminated the fol- lowing year. The ritual was certainly known in other parts of Christendom, for Egeria spoke of the Paschal vigil in Jerusalem as being "exactly as we observe it at home," although she notes that the Paschal flame in Jerusalem was taken from "within the grotto," that is, from the Lord's tomb. Nowhere does she indicate that the lamp-lighting itself was miraculous. Nonetheless, the opportunity to attend the Paschal cycle in Jerusalem was a coveted

Opposite: Interior of the Lord's Tomb.

event, for there the lucermarium (service of light) was enacted in the minia-ture church over Christ's Tomb, at the very place where the Lord had risen.

Almost fifty years before Egeria's pilgrimage, St. Constantine the Great, the first Christian Emperor, built a small, richly decorated sepulchre-chapel over the Lord's tomb. The original burial cave had been dug out of rock, and in order to enshrine the cave, the hill behind it was carefully chipped away until all that remained were the freestanding walls and roof enclosing the tomb.

In Greek, the small chapel is known as the *Kouklouvion*, and in English, the Edicule (from the Latin *aedicula*, meaning little house). The Edicule was made the center of the over-arching Church of the Holy Sepulchre, which also contains a number of churches, chapels, and the site of the crucifixion on Golgotha. The actual rock on which the Lord's body lay in the tomb was later covered by a marble slab, which pilgrims still kneel at today. Over this marble slab are hung dozens of oil lamps, with a larger lamp standing by itself on the marble. It is this lamp that is often the first to be ignited by the Holy Fire on the eve of Pascha.

There is no record of the Paschal flame ever appearing spontaneously outside of the Holy Sepulchre complex, and one wonders if the miraculous lighting didn't begin sometime after the consecration of the church in the fourth century. In other countries there was a prescribed order for the Paschal vigil, in which the clergy lit the "new fire" with flint and tinder, and then the Paschal candle. This was an integral part of the service, but it was never equated with the divinely-sent Fire in Jerusalem, which has always been acknowledged as uniquely miraculous. Indeed, for centuries these same churches made great efforts to transport the Paschal Fire from Jerusalem to Greece, Russia, Eastern Europe and the Middle East, overland and onboard ship, a practice that continued well into the twentieth century. It is now flown by airplane.

The history of the Holy Fire remains as mysterious as the Fire itself. There are no surviving narratives from early Christianity of supernatural prop-erties associated with either the Jerusalem flame or its yearly appearance. If the yearly *lucermarium* was already miraculous, it is perplexing why so noteworthy an event would have entirely escaped the pens of early pilgrims, non-Christian travelers, and the Church Fathers themselves. One narrative by Eusebius in his *History of the Church* does relate a Paschal miracle con-cerning Bishop Narcissus of Jerusalem (180-211), "thirtieth in line from the

Apostles." This story is not about the descent of the Holy Fire per se, but it is worth recounting as a miracle involving the Paschal lamps.

Once during the great all-night-long vigil of Easter, the deacons ran out of oil. The whole congregation was deeply distressed, so Narcissus told those responsible for the lights to draw water and bring it to him, and they obeyed him instantly. Then he said a prayer over the water, and instructed them to pour it into the lamps with absolute faith in the Lord. They again obeyed him, and, in defiance of natural law, by the miraculous power of God the substance of the liquid was physically changed from water into oil. All the years from that day to our own a large body of Christians there have preserved a little of it, as proof of that wonderful event.

Eusebius' reverence for the miracle in Jerusalem is so evident that it does not seem likely that he would have omitted the fact that the lamps were also lit by supernatural means, either at the time of Bishop Narcissus or a century and a half later when he wrote his history.

Likewise, although the writings of early Church Fathers such as Sts. Cyril of Alexandria and John Chrysostom often refer to light as a symbol of the grace and power of God, nowhere do they mention an annual miracle occurring at the Lord's tomb on Holy Saturday. Granted that multitudes of books and manuscripts were destroyed by fire, invasion, and the ruin of time, the large number of early writings we do have left are uniformly silent about miraculous events associated with the lamp-lighting. This does not mean that the Holy Fire had not yet begun to manifest. It simply means that we moderns do not have the evidence. We stand before the mystery as ignorant as any simple pilgrim of the past thousand years.

The first surviving accounts of otherworldly fire lighting the Paschal lamps are foreshadowed by ninth century lectionaries that specifically mention the Holy Fire by name (in Greek, "to Agion Phos," the Holy Light). Although these passages do not describe supernatural events, it is clear that they are referring to something worthy of reverence. The first description of the miraculous appearance of the Holy Fire is in 870, from a monk named Bernard, who writes in Latin, "an angel having come, light is lit in the lamps, which hang on the aforementioned Sepulchre."

An anonymous Moslem account of the late ninth century clearly describes the supernatural appearance of the Fire, and relates for the first time, that for some moments after its appearance the Fire does not burn those who touch it. It is an interesting sidelight that Arab-Moslem accounts of the descent of the Holy Fire are scattered throughout the following centuries, and to this day Moslems also attend the service.

One intriguing possibility is that if the Holy Fire did indeed begin to manifest in the eighth or ninth century when we first see eyewitness accounts, could this not have been a heavenly response to the iconoclasm that was threatening to overrun the Church? For two centuries, Christian iconoclasts attempted to force the Moslem-like exclusion of icons, frescoes, bas-reliefs, illuminated manuscripts, and other images of the Lord and His saints from worship. Because the Holy Fire descends only in the presence of the Orthodox patriarch or his representative – the argument continues – this may have been a Divine reaffirmation of the truth of traditional Orthodoxy. Certainly, Christians are not the only ones who devoutly receive the Holy Fire; it has fascinated centuries of Moslems as well.

With the exception of two hundred years of Crusader rule, the Holy Land remained in Islamic hands from 638, when Byzantine Jerusalem fell to the Arabs, until 1917 when it was freed from the Turks and placed under British mandate. This state of affairs made for unsettled relations between Jerusalem's Christians and their secular Islamic rulers. Many of the city's Moslem governors were tolerant of religious differences and came in state to attend the service of the Holy Fire. Others thought the miracle was a hoax. In 947 one Emir of Jerusalem complained that "...in performing your celebrated miracle with magic artifices, you have filled all of Syria with the religion of the Christians...." He intended to forbid the ceremony, but when advised of the revenues he would lose from the pilgrim trade he allowed the service to be held on condition that the Christians pay a huge compensation. The money was gathered, and as the service proceeded in the governor's presence, the entire church suddenly flooded with otherworldly light. A huge hanging lamp directly in front of the governor unaccountably drained its supply of oil and water, and then spontaneously ignited, albeit with nothing to burn.

Opposite: Orthodox altar on the Hill of Golgotha inside the Holy Sepulchre Church, Jerusalem.

In 1192, Saladin, the Saracen conqueror of Jerusalem, was so convinced that he had witnessed a fraud that he ordered the Paschal lamp in the Edicule blown out after the Holy Fire descended. As he watched, the lamp spontaneously relit. Again he ordered it blown out. Again it relit, and then a third time it lit again, to the joy of those gathered in the church.

A later and more destructive example of secular interference was the reign of the mad Caliph Al-Hakim (996-1021), a megalomaniac who impartially persecuted Christians, Jews and fellow-Muslims alike. According to Arab chroniclers, the popularity of the service of the Holy Light among both Christians and Moslems so infuriated Al-Hakim that he ordered the entire Holy Sepulchre complex leveled. Some historians believe his motives were in fact political, but in any event the holiest church in Christendom was destroyed and hundreds of others pillaged and ruined. At his succession, the Caliph's son El-Zahir (1021-1035) gave permission for the Holy Sepulchre to be rebuilt, but a lack of funds delayed the reconstruction for two decades. The Church was finally completed in 1042 under the patronage of Byzantine Emperor Constantine IX Monomachos. The Crusaders enlarged it when they took Jerusalem in 1099, and their renovated church is the one we see today.

Since its ninth-century appearance in written narratives, the miracle of the Holy Fire has been recounted hundreds of times in travel and religious literature. The outward form of the service today has much in common with that of early centuries.[1] First, the lamps are put out and the door of the Holy Sepulchre is sealed with wax to replicate the original sealing of the tomb with the stone. The Church is incensed with a procession around the Edicule. Finally, the patriarch of Jerusalem enters the tomb, while the people wait and pray in the darkened church. From the ninth century on, we have reports of the spontaneous lighting of the lamp on the tomb, from which the patriarch catches two large torches and thrusts them out of the sides of the Holy Sepulchre to the waiting crowd.

From the first attempts of Moslem rulers to prove that the descent of the Holy Fire was a hoax, a practice arose to insure the credibility of the Orthodox, which continues until now. After the lamps are put out on Saturday morning, the tomb is searched by Turkish guards to verify that

---

1 One difference from earlier centuries is the time of the lamp-lighting service. It was first held on Saturday night before the Paschal vigil, later moved to Saturday morning, and is now served in the early afternoon.

Opposite: Procession around Lord's Tomb with the customary Turkish guard.

there is nothing left inside with which to kindle a flame. The door of the tomb is then sealed with wax and left closed and guarded until the patriarch enters in the afternoon. Prior to breaking the seal, the patriarch himself is thoroughly searched by the guards and non-Orthodox clergy for matches or other implements. He then enters the Lord's Tomb, and prays kneeling until the Holy Fire descends.

Historically, those who accompany the Greek Orthodox patriarch have varied. From the ninth century narratives, it is apparent that Orthodox hierarchs from the West participated in the service along with Armenians and Copts. Even after the schism between the Greek East and the Latin West, Roman Catholic Crusaders ruling Jerusalem came to the service faithfully, praying with the Orthodox and receiving the sacred flame. The Holy Fire, however, descends only when the Greek Orthodox patriarch or his representative is in the tomb. Although the Holy Fire can descend before the patriarch enters, and once even appeared in the courtyard outside, it has never come down when a non-Orthodox hierarch was in the tomb alone.

Unfortunately, Roman Catholic participation came to an end in 1238 when Pope Gregory IX forbade Catholics to participate in the rite, declaring it a hoax. Unfortunately, it is impossible to evaluate the decision, as there are no surviving records detailing the pope's objection. Armenian and Coptic bishops in Jerusalem still play a major role in the service. In past centuries, the Armenian bishop has at times accompanied the Greek Patriarch as far as the narthex of the tomb. Presently, both the Armenian and the Coptic bishops wait outside the tomb. Once the Holy Fire descends, the Greek Orthodox patriarch passes torches to the Greek and Armenian bishops through specially designed openings near the front of the Holy Sepulchre; the Copts receive it seconds later. These hierarchs then distribute the Holy Fire to their own people. There has never been any Protestant representation.

Relations between the various Christian groups worshipping in the Holy Sepulchre have not always been harmonious, particularly in regard to Greek Orthodox preeminence. In 1580, Jerusalem's Armenian community promised the Moslem governor a large sum of money if he would prevent the Orthodox from entering the Church on Holy Saturday. He agreed, and at dawn, after the elated Armenians entered the Church, the doors were shut on the Orthodox, who remained in the courtyard with patriarch Sophronius IV. While the Armenians waited eagerly inside the Church, the disconsolate Orthodox continued to pray. Suddenly, one of the great stone columns at the door of the Holy Sepulchre split, and the Holy Fire sprang out of it. Thousands witnessed the miracle. After the Patriarch lit his own candle and those of the Orthodox present, the Moslem gatekeepers threw open the doors, and the Orthodox triumphantly marched in singing, "What God is as great as our God...." The split column still stands, and is pointed out to every pilgrim to Jerusalem.[2]

The local Arab population took the victory of the Orthodox so much to heart that every year young Arab men (usually Christian, but sometimes Moslem as well) celebrate the Orthodox regaining entrance to the church with an enthusiastic and unrestrained procession. In the hours preceding the descent of the Holy Fire, streams of young Arab men weave through the crowds. Sitting on one another's shoulders, they circle the Holy Sepulchre chanting, *Iesu Kum*! "Jesus is Risen!"–the Arab crowd responding with great vigor, *Hakkam Kum* "In Truth He is Risen!" Hour after hour the turbulent litany drowns out normal speech. Before the Patriarch enters on Saturday afternoon, one of the young Arabs, his eyes darkened with kohl, does a sword dance in front of the Holy Sepulchre with such flamboyant energy that it almost overshadows the Greek hierarchical procession that follows. A nun living in Jerusalem told the author that some years ago the Greek patriarch forbade the Arabs to do the sword dance. When the patriarch entered the tomb, however, the Holy Fire did not appear. The pilgrims waited anxiously for several hours, and it was only after the dance was allowed that the Holy Fire descended.

The appearance of the light can differ from year to year. Often it first manifests by the spontaneous lighting of the lamp on the Lord's Tomb. At other times it is seen in the air of the vast dome above the Lord's tomb as a ball of light or as miniature bolts of lightning before it descends to light the lamps. It can also appear as a cloud or smoke, and has even been seen as a cross of light. A few early witnesses insisted on it having come as a dove, or by the agency of an angel. Alternatively, it appears as a diffused light throughout the church, spontaneously lighting lamps or even pilgrims' candles seconds before (or after) the lamp in the Edicule is lit. Some years it is described as first having a bluish color; in others it is very bright red until finally subsiding into the appearance of a normal flame. Once it appears, it

2 It is also said that one of the Moslem gatekeepers, seeing the miracle, proclaimed Christianity as the true faith, for which he was immediately martyred by his fellow Turks.

takes only moments for the entire church to be lit, the flame passed candle by candle to thousands of pilgrims.

Antonios Stylianakis, a Greek Orthodox doctor, relates his impression: "My Lord, what was it? Torches, or an outbreak of fire? I thought that everything had caught fire! Within moments, it passed by me.... I leaned over to light my candle. Later, I learned that at different points, candles were being miraculously lit by themselves, so that in a short time the flame had spread everywhere, even outside the Church...Inside the Church some of the flames were over a meter high, because many people were holding bunches of candles in their hands."

For centuries, Jerusalem pilgrims have carried bundles of thirty-three candles, one for each year of the Lord's life. The flame of thirty-three wicks can be large indeed.

A remarkable characteristic of the Holy Fire is that for the first ten or fifteen minutes after its appearance, it does not burn. Pilgrims can hold it to their hands and faces (the author did so herself) with no more than a pleasantly warm sensation. While pilgrims first see the Fire appear in various ways, often depending on where they are standing in church, the short period in which the flame does not physically burn is experienced by everyone. After ten or fifteen minutes, the Fire becomes increasingly warm until it burns hot like any natural flame.

One of the most complete narratives of the descent of the Holy Fire was written in 1846 by Monk Parthenius, a Russian pilgrim. The following excerpt is his narration of the events of Holy Saturday in the Holy Sepulchre:

> When dawn came they began to put out the fire and lamps and nowhere was a lamp left burning. The Turks opened Christ's Sepulchre and put out all the lamps. Then the Turkish authorities and the Pasha himself came: a host of armed soldiers stood around Christ's Sepulchre. In the church everything had changed; everyone had become melancholy and the Arabs had become hoarse and weak. The church was unusually crowded and stuffy. Above, all the balconies were crammed with people in four rows. All the iconostasia and the domes were full of people. All were holding thirty-three candles in both hands in remembrance of the years of Christ's life. There was nothing lit anywhere.

Opposite: Detail of pillar with the crack from which the Holy Fire sprang out.

The Patriarch went up to the main iconostasis with the consul. Meletius, the Metropolitan of Trans-Jordan, sat in the altar with the rest of the bishops, all melancholy and hanging their heads. In the church the Moslems with their weapons of war were giving orders; the Arabs had already stopped running about, but stood lifting their hands to heaven and uttering compunctionate cries; the Christians were all weeping or continually sighing. And who at that time could withhold his tears, beholding such a multitude of people from all countries of the world weeping and wailing and asking mercy from the Lord God? It was joyous to see that now, although unwillingly, the rest of the Christians were showing some respect for the Orthodox Greek Faith and for the Orthodox themselves, and that they were looking upon the Orthodox as though upon the brightest of suns, because everyone was hoping to receive the grace of the Holy Fire from the Orthodox. The Armenian patriarch went to the altar with two bishops and the Coptic metropolitan, and they bowed to Metropolitan Meletius and the rest of the bishops and asked that when we receive the grace of the Holy Fire, that we grant it to them also. Metropolitan Meletius answered with humility and told them to pray to God. They went to their own places.

Then the royal gates were taken off and were replaced with others with a special opening. It is not possible to describe what was then happening in the church. It was as though all were waiting for the Second Coming of the King of Heaven. Fear and terror fell upon all, and the Turks became despondent. And in the church there was nothing to be heard except sighings and groans. And Metropolitan Meletius' face was wet with tears. Then the Turkish Pasha came with the other authorities, and they went into Christ's Sepulchre to make sure that nothing remained alight there. When they came out they sealed the Sepulchre, but previously they had placed a large lamp inside, filled to the very brim with oil. In it floated a large wick. They put the lamp in the middle of the Tomb of Christ. Now there were no Christians near the shrine, but only the Turkish authorities. And from the balconies they let down on ropes hundreds of wires with bunches of candles attached.

Opposite: One of two outlets from which the Patriarch of Jerusalem extends the torches lit by the Holy Fire to his left and right through the walls of the Holy Sepulchre to ignite the candles of those waiting in the church.

At eight o'clock according to Russian time (two in the afternoon), they began preparing for the procession with the Cross. The bishops, priests, and deacons, having dressed in all their sacred vestments, each took thirty-three unlit candles. Then from the altar, through the royal doors, were handed twelve banners, and whoever could took them. The soldiers cleared the way, and the chanters went behind the banners. From the altar through the royal doors came the deacons, priests, abbots and archimandrites, two by two, then the bishops, and behind all of them, Metropolitan Meletius. They went to the Lord's Sepulchre, and went around it three times chanting, "Thy Resurrection, O Christ our Saviour, the angels hymn in heaven; vouchsafe also us on earth with pure hearts to glorify Thee."

Having finished the procession, all the clergy went quickly into the altar with the banners. Metropolitan Meletius stayed alone at the entrance of the Sepulchre in the hands of the Turks. The Turks divested him, and the authorities searched him. Then they put the omophorion on him, opened the Sepulchre of Christ, and let him go inside. Oh, what fear and terror fell upon all them that were there at the time! All were silent and moaning and asking the Lord God that He not deprive them of the grace of His heavenly Fire. Some time passed. I do not know how long, for we were all beside ourselves from a kind of fear. But all of a sudden from near Christ's Sepulchre there shined a light. Soon light also appeared from the altar in the royal doors in the opening. And it flowed like two rivers of fire, one from the west, from Christ's sepulchre, and another from the east, from the altar. Oh, what joy and exultation there was in church then! Everyone became as though drunk or beside himself, and we did not know who was saying what, or who was running where! And a great noise rose in all of the church. All were running around, all were crying out in joy and thanksgiving – most of all the Arab women. The Turks themselves, the Moslems, fell on their knees and cried, "Allah, Allah," that is, "O God, O God!" Oh, what a strange and most wonderful sight! The whole church was transformed into fire. Nothing could be seen in the church besides the heavenly Fire. Above and below, and round all the balconies the Holy Fire was being poured forth. And afterwards there was smoke about the whole church. And a good half of the people went out with the Fire and carried it about Jerusalem to their own homes and to all the monasteries.

...In Jerusalem I heard from many people with whom the Metropolitan himself had spoken about it openly, "Sometimes I go in and it is already burning; then I take it out quickly. But sometimes I go in and the lamp is not yet burning; then I fall down to the ground from fear and begin with tears to beg mercy from God. When I get up the lamp is already burning and I light two bunches of candles and carry them out and distribute them..."

With an increase of travelers from the West after the seventeenth century, we have many non-Orthodox accounts of the service from English, Continental and American witnesses. With few exceptions, they are unvaryingly disgusted by the Arab dancing, appalled by the deep faith of the crowd, and damn the appearance of the Holy Fire as "an infernal hoax." They explain that the fraud is wrought by the Greeks alone, the Greeks and Armenians together, or of the Turks in connivance with the Greeks. Never, by any possibility, could it be a miracle.

What never occurs to these critics is that their "hoax" has been maintained for well over a thousand years. Certainly it is a record in the history of mankind. This also presupposes at least eleven centuries of fraudulent Greek Patriarchs, not one of whom had the integrity to reveal the "secret" of the Holy Fire or deny its miraculous origin, even, presumably, when assiduously bribed. (Not to mention the remarkably consistent record of "secrecy" among the Greek priests, deacons and monks serving at the Holy Sepulchre who would have been party to the conspiracy – some of whom, like St. Gerasimos of Cephalonia, are canonized saints.)

Secondly, these narrators neglect to take into account the many attempts by the Moslem rulers of Jerusalem to discredit the Holy Fire, all of which were unsuccessful. Nor do they consider that relations between the Orthodox, Armenians and Roman Catholics have often been rocky at best. Who would more diligently work to uncover a fraud than these fellow-Christians, both in the interest of plain truth and to extend their own influence over the Holy Places? And what about the years in which the Armenian hierarch accompanied the Greek Patriarch as far as the narthex of the tomb, from where (three feet away) he would certainly have observed any artificial means of lighting the lamp? Finally, not one of these travelers

has ever admitted to making the simple experiment of taking a newly lit candle into his own hands immediately after the descent of the Holy Fire to see if it burned him. The critics disgrace their own reasoning. Let us leave them to their grumbling.

... The Arabs suddenly appear again on each other's shoulders, shouting and crying, "Iesu Kum! Hakkam Kum! This time they stop in front of the Lord's Tomb. A youth with kohl-blackened eyes jumps out from their midst, waving two swords in a passionate dance. There is something archaic about him, like the wild, lamenting energy of the Old Testament. I think of David dancing before the Ark. He finishes and is carried away on the shoulders of his Arab brothers. Suddenly the doors of the Church open to admit the Patriarch and the Jerusalem clergy in procession. They incense the church and circle the Tomb, coming to a halt after the third turn. The crowd watches silently as the Patriarch is searched for matches. As the guards unseal the door I look up into the dome. High above me I see what look like small flashes of lightning in the air. I whisper to Irina, asking what she sees. She sees it as well, and others around us begin to point and exclaim. Finally the Patriarch enters the Tomb. The crowd is now silent, even the Arabs, and together we await the Holy Fire. Moments pass. There is darkness in the tomb and silence in the crowd. An old woman near me whispers in Russian, "Gospody Pomiloi!" (Lord, have mercy!). The Greeks behind us echo, "Kyrie Eleison!" and one of them begins to weep. I wonder if this is what it will be like on Judgment Day – an immense crowd of people, holding our breaths in fear and hope, waiting on the Lord.

Suddenly there is a triumphant shout from the front of the crowd. We see a light in the Tomb, and torches are thrust out. The Holy Fire has come! The anxious faces become radiant. It is Pascha. Strangers hug one another; we are all brothers in our joy. I think, "This too, will be at the Last Judgment." It is only a moment before our own candles are lit – the sacred flame passed to us by the Romanians who shouted in the night. I put my hand over it. As they

Opposite: The patriarch of Jerusalem passing the Holy Fire to waiting worshippers.

said, it doesn't burn! I touch the flame to my face, my hair – it is always the same, a wondrous warm light. Israeli policemen stand on the ledges of the pillars with fire extinguishers, putting out the candles they can reach. They are afraid of fire with so many pilgrims, but they, too, have caught the joy of the crowd. No matter. The candles are easily relit. The light will never go out. It is eternal. It is a miracle. He is Risen.

– N. Tikhonova ✤

Bibliography

Eusebius, *The History of the Church*, Penguin Classics, New York, 1965.

Egeria: Diary of a Pilgrimage, (Ancient Christian Writers #38), Ed. Burghardt, Paulist Press, 1970.

Freeman-Grenville, G.S.P, *The Holy Land*, Continuum, NY, 1996.

Kallistos, Archimandrite, "The Holy Fire," *Orthodox Life*, Vol. 34 #2 (1984) Jordanville, NY.

Parthenius, Monk, "Holy Week and Pascha in Jerusalem," *Orthodox Life*, Vol. 34, #2 (1984), Jordanville, NY.

Auxentios, Bishop, *The Paschal Fire in Jerusalem*, St. John Chrysostomos Press, Berkeley, CA, 1995.

Stylianakis, M.D., Antonios, "I Saw With My Own Eyes the Holy Light," unpublished manuscript.

Tikhonova, N. N., unpublished journal, Moscow, 1997.

TEACHING OUR CHILDREN TO PRAY

Reflections of a Young Mother

When the *Road to Emmaus* staff first decided to talk to an Orthodox mother about children and prayer we pictured an experienced woman with grown-up children and the leisure for a long interview. After some discussion, however, we decided on Inna Belov, a young mother with a three-year-old son, "in the midst of the fray." At a time when her joys, fears and concerns about raising an Orthodox child occupy most of her waking hours, we found Inna's spontaneous reflections both fresh and intriguing.

RTE: Inna, Can you tell us a little about your background?

INNA: Yes. I was raised in Moscow, and after secondary school I attended the Moscow Institute of Foreign Languages. I wasn't baptized until I became very ill at the age of nineteen. After my baptism I recovered within a half a year, and began going to church regularly. I worked as a receptionist, and at Valaam Podvoriye in Moscow selling candles. I married my husband Victor when I was twenty-nine and had Nicholas when I was thirty-two. Nicholas is now three.

My husband Victor grew up in a non-believing family and became Orthodox at the age of twenty-three or twenty-four after his friends brought him to church. He is an artist and worked for many years frescoing churches. After we were married, however, he didn't want to leave us for long periods to paint, so he got work in Moscow as a graphic designer and later went to school to become an accountant. We are hoping he may be ordained soon.

Opposite: Inna Belov and her son Nicholas.

RTE: What about your family? Were they believers?

INNA: My two grandmothers were very simple. They believed in God, but in such a natural fashion that no one noticed. There is a story about my grandmother Maria, who once was very late coming home. When she finally arrived my parents asked her, "Why did you take so long?" She said, "I had to walk a long way." "Why?" "Because I didn't have any money to pay the fee on the trolley." "But why? You can go without any fee, because they seldom check the tickets." "Yes, but I thought it probably was a sin." That was what she was like. Maria died when I was three.

My other grandmother, Alexandra – my mother's mother – always brought us Easter eggs and kulich for Pascha. I remember it very well. She would sit in the kitchen and talk for a long time about her children and grandchildren. She couldn't hear anything, but she was able to speak. I have a clear picture of her sitting in the kitchen, with the Paschal sun shining through the window and resting like a blessing on the eggs and kulich. It was like a moment out of paradise.

When my grandmother Alexandra died, I knew she believed the soul lives on because she said to me, "Come and see me off." One of her grandsons had bought her a burial shroud as a present, with Orthodox words and crosses on it. It was very rare thing in those days and she often brought it out to show people, saying, "Look what I have." She looked forward to her death with a peaceful heart. In 1992 her great-grandson was born weak and sickly, the doctors said he wouldn't live. When Alexandra was told she replied, "I am so old...I want to die in his place, so he will live." She was eighty-three and in extremely good health, but three weeks later she died with no warning. That same day, the baby began to recover. He was born on the seventeenth of December and she died on the eighth of January.

In spite of all this, I was not a believer. I was against religion because of all the atheist propaganda I had been taught in school, in Pioneer camps, everywhere. When at nine, my father said something one day about God. I was astonished and said, "How can you say this? It's lerigion." I didn't even know how to say the word "religion," but I already knew how to fight against it. Then, when I was fourteen I had a teenage crisis. I saw a cross around my mother's neck, a little Orthodox cross, and I asked her to let me see it. She did, and suddenly I became so angry with her for being ignorant and unmodern that I threw it out the window. She went downstairs and tried to find the cross in the snow, but she couldn't. Afterwards she never said anything to me about it. I don't know if she went to church then. I don't think so, but she had the kind of natural faith that you just get from the air.

RTE: Why do you think your parents didn't talk to you about God or religion when you were a child? Was it because they knew it would only lead to trouble for you in school, or were they still not sure of their own faith?

I don't think they realized that they should speak to me about it, because they had a kind of faith without knowledge. They knew they believed in God, but they didn't know any church dogma. They didn't know anything. They were baptized as infants, and they believed in God and in the Church, but they didn't know they should go there every Sunday. Atheist propaganda was so powerful that you didn't hear a single word about God outside the church. Even in church the priests couldn't say whatever they wanted. They could only serve. They sometimes gave short sermons, but they were not allowed to instruct. Those who preached with conviction were persecuted.

RTE: Before she died last year, I remember your mother as being rather devout.

INNA: Yes, during her last two months she received Holy Communion almost every week. Before that she had begun going to church, and by the time she died her prayer book was ragged from having been used so much. My parents were wedded in the church at age sixty, at my request, but my mother said, "If I am going to go through with this, please don't have anyone else there." My father is devout, but he is very slow in acquiring Orthodox knowledge. It's still difficult for him to understand about the Trinity, about Christ being both God and man. He's always asking me about these things and I try to explain. He is a very simple soul, like my mother and my grandmothers.

The priests now say that our generation is different from the previous ones. Before, parents and grandparents brought their children to the Church. Now it is the children who bring their parents. However, it was not that way for me. As little as they knew of religion, it was my parents who brought me to the Church. When I became very ill at nineteen, the doctors could do nothing for me. My parents took me to a priest and had me baptized, hoping it would help. It was only after I was baptized that I began to recover.

RTE: Before your child was born, had you thought of how you would begin to teach him about God, how to pray? Did you have the example of an older friend?

INNA: No, I had to think about all this myself. I wanted so much to be a mother that I prayed to God, "Please give me a baby and I will try to bring him up Orthodox." I try hard not to forget this. I asked only that the baby would be healthy and have a good loving heart to love God.

As soon as I found out that I was going to have a child, and even before, when I was praying for one, I knew that I wanted to inspire in him my own love for Christ. I didn't think much about teaching him to pray, or bringing him to church. The love of Christ was the main thing I wanted to give him. Now it is a little more difficult and different from what I thought, but that was my first idea.

In regards to this, I also think of Archbishop Anthony Bloom's words to parents who ask him about bringing up children, "I cannot give advice relying on my own experience because I was not a believing child." It is difficult for me for the same reason, and this is why I have to bring Nicholas up as a young adult, from an adult point of view. If he has any faith it will not be childish faith. Of course, from his side it will be a childish faith, but what comes from me will give him a sort of adult faith. I'm afraid there might even be something of a distortion here, because I cannot penetrate what he sees, never having had the experience myself.

Later it will be important for him to have friends who are older, and who have gone through all these early periods as Orthodox Christians. Particularly during his teen-age years I want him to have older friends who have been brought up Orthodox.

RTE: Many people feel that children are naturally devout – that is, until the world creeps in and clouds their souls. Did you see any indication of this in your child when he was small?

INNA: Yes, many indications. Soon after he was born we would put an icon of the Mother of God in front of him. He would smile and wave his hands, look at her and sort of speak to her. He wasn't like this with toys or other pictures we put in front of him. Afterwards, when we began to take him to church and taught him to pray he was very zealous and even made prostrations to the floor. He was only two. If one of us skipped anything in the morning or evening prayers, he would protest and say, "You missed this prayer, please say it." But, you know, when I heard this I thought I was on my way to having my own little church babushka – a two-year-old babushka. I felt sick. So, I decided to try something different. Not to make things so very strict and in order, but to accent things that are connected with prayer. For example, I try to connect the life that he leads as a Christian with the life that he leads in the world, with other children, with me at home...

RTE: And you did this because you felt that even at two years old, he was getting bound up in externals?

INNA: I think what he was doing was natural, but after I saw what was happening I began to pray more prayers that concerned our life. For example, I would say aloud to God, "Let us live this day without any quarrels, let Nicholas and I have peace between ourselves, that he might be kind to me and I might be kind to him."

RTE: How early did you begin to teach him to pray?

INNA: The only thing I could do when he was a baby, of course, was to pray myself in his presence.

RTE: He watched you from the crib?

INNA: Yes, we only have one room and he was always here, so he heard me pray. As he got older, he joined me when he wanted to. I always make a point of him saying a prayer for his reposed grandmother whom he loved, and whose funeral he attended a few months ago, and for us, his parents, because this is what he understands.

RTE: Does he know any prayers by heart?

INNA: He can say the "Our Father" and the "Theotokos and Virgin Rejoice." He has been doing it since he turned two. One day he recited a poem to me, and when I saw that he already remembered things by heart I asked him, "Please say the "Our Father," and he did. "Please say "Theotokos and Virgin Rejoice," and he did. He already knew them, but it hadn't occurred to him to say them. (Unfortunately, his diction was so bad that only I could understand them.) Now he also knows "O Heavenly King..." and "Holy God, Holy Mighty, Holy Immortal...."

Although he has memorized these prayers, I think that he still pronounces them mechanically. He says them from his heart, certainly, but he doesn't understand the meaning. Once I tried to explain to him, "Please forgive us our trespasses, as we forgive those who trespass against us." I explained to him what sin is and then later, when I raised my voice and scolded him, he said, "Don't shout at me, it is a sin." I thought then that I probably wasn't the person to teach him about sin. (Laughs) The only thing I could answer was, "Please don't wrack my nerves because that is a sin too."

Also, I ask him to pray for people if they have asked. Sometimes people say to me, "If you pray, it doesn't mean much. Let the innocent baby pray for me." And I say, "Please pray for Aunt Lena. She asked us to. Let us say, 'God have mercy on Aunt Lena,'" and he says it. Or, "Please pray that Uncle Andrew's work goes well." Things like that. Or, "Please pray that you can forgive your friend Steve for taking away your pail." (If he cannot, for example.) In this way, we have taught him to forgive joyfully. He likes to forgive people. When someone asks his forgiveness, he smiles with a great, wide smile and says, "Certainly, I forgive you." Before the person asks for forgiveness he will cry and be nasty and upset – but as soon as they ask, why yes, it is granted, everything's OK – even if they've just hit him with a toy spade.

RTE: When do you think he began to understand about forgiveness?

INNA: I think he understood as soon as I began to ask his forgiveness. I am always asking his forgiveness. Sometimes, once, twice, three times a day I raise my voice at him. Sometimes I spank him. If I spank him too hard, I ask him to forgive me. Sometimes he comes to me and says, "Mama, please forgive me." "For what?" "I don't know, for something." Or, he'll come to me and say, "Mama, thank you." "For what?" "For everything." He is so funny.

RTE: Does he join you in your morning and evening prayers? Do you think this is important?

INNA: It is important for him to be present, and not to shout, not to run about. If he is drawing in the corner, and listening with one ear, I think that's all right. If I want him to say a prayer, I call him and ask him to.

RTE: How do you get him to pay attention when he is at family prayers? What do you do if he becomes bored and restless?

Opposite: Victor, Inna and Nicholas Belov.

INNA: If he becomes restless I understand that he is just a little child, and let him do whatever he wants, as long as it doesn't interfere with my prayers. Sometimes when he doesn't want to say his prayers, I ask him, "Please come help me because I am tired. Please help me to say this prayer."

RTE: At what point will you start asking him to stand with you and be attentive?

INNA: I think that I will do it gradually. For example, if he says one or two prayers during our morning prayers now, in a month I will ask him to say three prayers... He is still so young that I have to draw his attention to every prayer we say, and it must be short. What is important is that there is a large icon of Christ before him, so that he knows to Whom he is praying. We have a big poster of Christ the Saviour with large eyes, and we have a poster of the Mother of God. Maybe this is not right, certainly it is not Christ Himself, but I think it helps him to understand.

RTE: Was there a time when you saw prayer start to become a habit, where Nicholas didn't want to do without it? Does he ever pray by himself or does he always have to be reminded?

INNA: It differs. Sometimes he wants to pray. If he wants to pray he doesn't ask me to pray, he just prays by himself. In the morning if I don't remind him he won't remember. During the day he will, but not in the morning or in the evening. But what he does remember is to bless his father and his grandfather when they leave the flat. He says, "In the name of the Father, and of the Son, and of the Holy Spirit," and makes a little cross over them.

He says a few regular prayers, like, "God have mercy on my reposed Granny." He does this without my being there. Of course, we always bless the food together, and say the prayer of thanksgiving afterwards. When I leave him alone while I'm working in our small kitchen, he sometimes becomes lonely and will say a prayer. Also he will sometimes pray in difficult situations. For example, once I was speaking with a friend about a person that I couldn't forgive from my heart. Nick, hearing me, began to say the "Our Father." It was when he was two and a half. My friend connected it with the situation, but I don't know if it was really so. Probably the baby just felt that there was something wrong, and decided to pray.

Sometimes, people speaking to Nicholas have an idea that as a child he is supposed to be more innocent and more devout than adults. A few times, when people came to visit us he felt that attitude, and began to pray to attract attention. I didn't like it. It wasn't natural, but we have tried to do something about it. Now, he understands that praying is a serious thing between us and God and not something to be demonstrated.

Something else is happening now. When Nicholas prays for our family he says, "God have mercy on Mama, on Papa, on grandpa, on my godmother, and on the mouse." He calls himself, "mouse." It has been a very long-lasting game. When people ask him his name he says, "My name is mouse." When he prays, he prays for "the mouse." I don't know what to do about it. Nicholas calls me Mama Myshka, "the mouse's mother," and Victor, "the mouse's father." When his godmother comes, he says, "Here we are, all the mice together." I hope it doesn't offend his patron saint, because I don't seem to be able to stop him.

There is something else I am thinking about here as well. This is not really about prayer, but it concerns young children. It is about drinking holy water and eating prosphora. Nick does it with joy. We try to do it every morning. One mother told me that she brought up her child on water from

St. Sergius holy spring, and that during the day she often gives him holy things to kiss, etc. There was such a fantastic result in her child that I think this is the only thing I can do regularly for Nick at this age without an awful effort. I try to do it too, and I can say that I see some results.

RTE: What kind of results do you see?

INNA: I see very clear results in his disposition. He becomes more reasonable, happier, calmer. I try to do it as often as I can. Every morning I anoint him with holy oil. But I try not to make these things fixed so that he won't think they are tasks to be performed at certain times, and that they can only be done like this and no other way. I think this is important, and it is why I try to read different prayers aloud when he is standing beside me and listening. I choose different prayers from the Morning Prayers every day, so that he will not think that prayers are some logarithm to memorize by which you can pray without thinking. I try to anoint him, or give him holy water to drink or an icon to kiss whenever I remember. I do it when I have spare time during the day because I think it is the only way for a relaxed mother like myself to keep up his faith.

Sometimes, if I am busy in the kitchen and he is restless, I will sit him on the sofa with the prayer rope in his hand and he will say, "Lord have mercy" with each knot. It is repetitive and easily understood. I think small children like things like that. And he knows somehow that he is doing something real.

RTE: Can you recall any of Nicholas' prayers that particularly touched you?

INNA: He doesn't pray with his own words, but he repeats the prayers that he has heard me say. I expected him to pray, "Please make mother be kinder," but he doesn't. He says, "Please let us live this day in peace." He is already a diplomat.

When he was younger he would line his stuffed animals up with their faces before the icons. He wouldn't pray or say anything, but he would stand with them quietly. I think he thought they were praying. He put his cars there also, but we explained to him that cars don't pray, and so he took them away.

RTE: Does he have a sense of the saints yet?

INNA: He has a sense of saints because of the books we've been reading to him about saints, but mainly he prays to the Lord, the Mother of God, and to St. Nicholas, his patron saint.

RTE: Do you feel that a child's spiritual growth is something that happens naturally, as long as there aren't crude or worldly influences around him, or is it something that takes step by step guidance from you?

INNA: I think that my child's spiritual growth is closely connected with my behavior. If I myself am convinced that God listens to my prayers, if I myself really lead a spiritual life, it will naturally be imprinted on the child. But if I pray without conviction I don't think it will have any influence on him. The most important thing is that I am determined and sincere myself. Otherwise it is impossible. I believe that even if I never taught him anything, if I only prayed and he could feel that I was praying, it would be enough.

RTE: Yes, That is a good point, and during the Soviet period there were people who believed, but didn't feel they could teach about Christianity or even pray outwardly, for fear that their children would say something in school that would cause problems for the family. Yet many of those children, who are now adults, have told me that they had a kind of natural faith, that they imbibed quietly from believing relatives and sometimes "from the air."

INNA: Yes, I have stories like that about my husband Victor. His grandfather's brother was a priest in the Ivanovo region in Kineshma. We think he must have prayed for Victor from heaven, because Victor's parents are not believers. He remembers, though, that before his Granny died, she showed him an icon and said, "Look, this is God." He was about seven, and he remembers that quite clearly.

Victor's mother is a convicted atheist. In spite of this, he didn't grow up as an atheist. When he was ten his mother began taking him to Tretyakov Gallery. He would stand in front of the icons for hours until she dragged him away, saying, "What do you see in those things?"

Later he went to a Young Pioneer camp [a Communist youth summer camp]. There was a teacher there who taught them to draw pictures and make all sorts of images on metal and wood. He chose to do a relief of a monk in copper – he had seen a picture of one in an art book. *(Inna points to the metal relief above our heads in the kitchen, a rather sophisticated looking piece of art.)*. I think that, taking into account he was only twelve, it is a rather pious work. I don't think the Pioneer leader saw it though. Victor just took it home. He wasn't baptized until he was in his twenties, when his friends brought him to church, but he says that on the day he was baptized he felt that he was really changed.

There are many life problems bound up with disbelief in families. For example, I don't know what I will do when Nicholas begins to play with unbelieving children – if he talks to them about God, or prays in their presence. But no such problem has arisen yet. People say that children understand that even if they believe in God other people are not obliged to, and they take it naturally.

RTE: I think children are often aware of the subtlety of people's responses. If someone doesn't respond in the way you're used to, you just realize that there are people you can't talk to about such things.

INNA: Yes. I also foresee situations like the following. I know of a little girl who believes in God. One day her Granny took her to music school and they had to go by tram. The tram didn't come for a long time and this unbeliev-

ing Granny looked at her and said, "Why don't you pray that your God sends us this tram."

RTE: Have you thought about how you would explain to Nicholas about praying for things like that and then not getting them?

INNA: I'm sure I can explain how he may not get something extra, something that he wants but doesn't need. Probably I could say something like, "Are you sure that if your prayer is granted that this tram will not have an accident because it is going too fast?" Or, "Perhaps there is an old woman who also needs to catch it, and if it comes more quickly she will not be in time." Also, "We are not the only people who want the tram to come. There are hundreds waiting along this route."

However, it will be much harder to explain if he prays for a friend to get well and the child doesn't. Of course, I know the answers that are given in such cases. I know that God has His own ways, that He doesn't see the situation as we do, and that He knows what is best for us, but I cannot say this to Nicholas with conviction. It is not that I don't believe it, but I don't have enough of what I would call the "energy of faith" to transfer it. Probably I should take him to a priest for this, to someone who has that faith. Until I have it myself, I will just have to honestly say, "I don't know." If I can't transfer it with conviction, it will sound empty to him.

RTE: Do you foresee other things that atheists might do or say to influence him?

INNA: Many unbelieving parents repeat parrot-like from atheist propaganda. For example, they say that Christianity is the religion of weak people. I plan to tell Nicholas that that is true; we are all weak people. If we were strong people we could keep away disease, death and sorrow, but we cannot. Let's not conceal it. Christianity is the religion of weak people because everyone is weak. It's for all of us. Of course, there are strong people – but they are saints. Christianity is a religion for everyone, whether you are weak or strong.

As for other things atheists might say, their arguments used to be simpler: "Cosmonauts flew into space and they saw no angels, no God, nothing."

Opposite: Nicholas Belov.

Now atheism has become very clever. I think this is a good thing because it is a challenge that one has to meet.

RTE: Does Nicholas' prayer-life at home carry over to church?

INNA: I know I am not right, but I still only take him to church for Holy Communion. When I take him to church I don't take him to long services – our Sunday service from beginning to end is about six hours. I take him at other times to stand for awhile when there aren't many people there. Every day that we go out for a walk we stop at the church. We pray, or I say, "Let's just stand and listen and watch," for him to feel something if he can. Certainly he likes to light candles, to make the sign of the cross, to bow, to kiss the icons. Sometimes he spontaneously prays at the corner where they place candles for the reposed. But he prays so loudly – he cries right out, "Lord have mercy on my grandmother." (Laughing) I get embarrassed. He just doesn't notice that there are other people there.

So far, I am glad that Nicholas prays and bows and crosses himself, that he places candles, and kisses icons with joy. I think that's the main thing, to not make him feel disgust. I am still sorry though, that I can't take him to the whole service.

RTE: Isn't it common in Russia to wait until very young children are older? Particularly since you have such bitter winters, freezing waits for the tram, long walks to church, and eight long flights of stairs to get the baby, baby stroller, and groceries up to the flat. The churches being crowded also make it difficult. From what I've seen it is rather usual for mothers not to take their young children to church except for Holy Communion, and then as they get older they attend more regularly.

INNA: Yes. Maybe it is wrong, but I am weak in this. It is a podvig for me to take a very young child to services and stand there with him for hours. Of course, it might be different if you have taken him to services every day since he was born, but I was simply not capable of this. I adore the people who have three, four or five children and who bring them to church all together. It looks fantastic. Having one child I know what it is like, but having three or four young ones.... The children from these families might move about a bit, venerate the icons or place a candle, but they don't run about or gather into little groups and talk. Mothers sometimes even bring their babies in knapsacks and baby carriages.

RTE: It's different for everyone.

INNA: I think that a mother who has a lot of children is like an angel in a fresco by Michaelangelo. It's really a gift. Of course, God helps too. I can't imagine what really pious and strong mothers will think of me after reading what I've said, but I ask them to be condescending.

RTE: What have you learned from watching your son pray?

INNA: Frankly speaking, nothing particularly good. I see my mistakes in the spiritual life – I hear my tone of voice in him, and understand that in some ways I am too emotional, in other ways I am too formal...I see the reflection of all of this in him. When I ask him to pray to Christ in front of this large icon, I do see a sort of awe in him. It is probably the only good thing. Mainly I see my mistakes.

One thing I have learned is how responsive children's hearts are and how quickly they turn to God. As adults, even when we know something is right, we often hesitate. We move slowly, first weighing the cost. Children are different. When I tell Nicholas, "Pray to God and tell Him that you love Him, and that you know He loves you," he immediately makes a prostration and prays. There is only one second between my words and his action. When he stands carelessly in front of the icons, I say, "Stand up straight and quiet so that God will know you are seriously praying." He immediately obeys. He responds from his heart without any hesitation.

RTE: Is there anything else you wanted to say about children and prayer in general?

INNA: My problem is in connecting prayer with life. For example, I do not tell Nicholas to pray if he wants a new game or a toy. I can't tell him to ask God, because I know that I am going to buy it. If there is something that I don't think I can do for him, I also don't want to tell him to pray, because I am afraid he will be disappointed. I don't have enough faith myself. But I do want him to pray for his own state of mind. For example, "God, let me be peaceful, God help me to forgive this person," and so on. I know that God wills to give him forgiveness and peace of mind, but I am not sure about the toys. I don't want him to become a devout young person because he thinks that he can get whatever he wants if he prays.

Again, about connecting prayer to life, there is a story I once read by a priest. He said, "When I was a young child and I disobeyed, my simple-hearted Mother knelt in front of the icons and prayed, sometimes with tears, 'See, God, see how badly my child is treating me. Help me.' This always made me stop what I was doing."

But I think you can be too disciplined as well. One of our friends had his first child right after he was converted. When the child was very young and ran off in another direction in church, or stood in a place where he was not supposed to be, he took him by the ear and dragged him away. The boy grew up nervous. With the second child, he was less strict and the child is more devout.

RTE: What do you think is the lesson from that?

INNA: I just thank God that I didn't have Nicholas when I first converted, when I was new and zealous. I think that a child should feel free with God. Maybe this just concerns, my child, but because I believe that he needs to feel at ease with people, I also think he needs to feel at ease with God and to feel free to do what he wants as long as it doesn't contradict some moral guideline. For example, I don't spank him if he grabs an icon and carries it in his hand quite impiously. I just take it away, put it where it should be, and tell him not to do it again. I know that some people are very strict with their children in those situations, but I don't think it is right.

My point is that I don't want Nicholas to feel that God and his mother are his enemies, that we are aligned against him. Also, I don't want him to have to flee to God from his family and friends. I want us all to be united. I think that my main purpose in the family is to make sure that none of us are in opposition to the others. I'm speaking of myself here because Nicholas' father is often absent working. He comes late and leaves early, so I am with the baby during most of his waking hours.

RTE: What do you see as your husband's part in Nicholas' spiritual life?

INNA: We think it is very important for the father to take part. There was an investigation conducted in atheist times so that they could better fight against religion, about children from believing homes. They found that where the father believes in God and goes to church, about ninety percent of the children become religious, but when it is just the mother, only ten percent do. I don't know if it is the same for a democratic society, but I believe there is something to think about here.

When Victor is here, he does pray with him of course. What is important is that Nicholas sees him praying.

RTE: If Victor is ordained, as you hope, then Nicholas will have time with him in church, and within a few years he will be his altar attendant.

INNA: Yes, but I'll tell you something that I'm afraid of for him, something that I've noticed among young altar attendants, even among some children of the clergy. They will often tell you where you can place a candle, or where you should stand, etc. I don't mean all priests' children – some of them are wonderful. Nevertheless, I do see a few imitating the behavior of their elders without the content or authority. They begin to look down on people. Not only other children, whom they try to boss around, but on older people as well. I never want my son to tell an older person what to do in church. I want him to stay in his place, to understand that he is just a little child. I do not allow him to make comments on older people's behavior. (I don't mean mine, I know mine is imperfect).

RTE: Can we go back to the idea of connecting prayer with life? Did you have anything more to say about this?

INNA: Yes. This also concerns very young children. To connect prayer with life, I think a baby should feel that the main thing in faith is mercy. We try to inspire this mercy in Nicholas all day long.

We hope that later it will be connected with faith. So far we have not succeeded in connecting it. For example, when his friend cries, on the way home I ask, "Why do you think he cried? What do you think his mood was? Do you think it was bad or good? Why?" I ask him to try to notice how a person feels. I think this is the only kind of mercy he is capable of so far, since he cannot physically help anyone. Helping me in the kitchen is really a game, and he feels it. But having psychological mercy on people is already not a game for him. For example, when his friend wants one of Kolya's toys, and he doesn't give it to him, I don't say, "You are being greedy. Don't be greedy." I try to explain that this toy attracts his friend because it is new to him. I try to make him understand how the other person sees it.

By mercy I mean taking into account the other person, because children usually don't do this. This is not the core of mercy, but it is the mechanism – taking into account the other person's feelings, his situation. For adults, probably, the core of mercy is wishing another person's salvation and not interfering with the process. Helping it as you can. Helping a person with his physical needs is very simple for us, but for a child it is difficult. Handing over alms that his mother gives him for beggars, "helping" her carry a heavy bag, is all a sort of game. He cannot really help anyone except through her, but he can begin to take care of people psychologically. Just this week, I saw a result of this in Nicholas. He came into the kitchen and asked me what I was doing. I said, "I am making a special tea for our neighbor because she is ill." He said, "Then we must go pray for her." That, I think, is hopeful.

I have heard people say, "You must do this because God wants you to." We are going to say it in the future, but I'm afraid to mention God in that way right now because I do not yet live a life closely connected with these things myself. For example, I don't pray every hour. When I speak to people I do not always consider how God sees the situation. But as soon as I begin to connect more moments in my own life with this remembrance of God, I hope to be able to connect this mercy we are trying to plant in our son with faith in God. Then I will be able to convey to him that God indeed wants this. I hope that these two things will coincide.

RTE: Don't you also think, that as a soul learns human mercy and human kindness, it will naturally lead it to an understanding of God's mercy, which is much greater?

INNA: I think so. I think that from early childhood a young person should feel that above all, God is merciful. And to feel it he has to be merciful himself and to understand what mercy is. If not, then when he is ten and we tell him that God is merciful, he won't understand. We want him to have this early childhood impression that God is not only Who you pray to, that God is not this or that, but that God is mercy. I think all the rest can be done afterwards. Mercy is like kindness, but kindness is a natural thing, while mercy can be instilled.

I have to say that I am only repeating what comes to mind. By no means do I think that I am doing these things. I only say them aloud because I cannot stop myself from thinking about what concerns me. When I read or hear such reflections or speculations – "this is like this, and that is like that," it always makes me wonder. I know that I am not at all authorized to speak about mercy. It is awful to speak about mercy and yet not really be merciful myself, but I do want my child to have this quality, so I have to think about it sometimes. I hope that the people reading this will forgive me. ✢

FROM AMERICA TO RUSSIA

The Myrrh Streaming Icon of Tsar Nicholas II

By Richard (Thomas) Betts

A myrrh-streaming icon of Tsar Nicholas II has appeared in Russia, and it appeared with the same unpretentious simplicity with which the late Tsar abdicated his throne and bore his final months of house arrest. The icon was not painted by a contemporary iconographer in Moscow or St. Petersburg, nor is it the property of one of the old and venerable churches. It is, in fact, an inexpensive paper copy of an American icon, given away in Russia by the thousands by a Russian-American wife and mother, Ija Schmit, the founder of the Society Honoring Russian Nobility.[1]

Shortly after her mother passed away in 1995, Ija began pondering how to spend the small inheritance that she had been left in her mother's will. One night in September she awakened to the thought that she should use it to have an icon painted of Tsar-Martyr Nicholas. The icon would be dedicated to the future canonization of Tsar-Martyr Nicholas in Russia, and in memory of her mother.

After Ija's initial inspiration to have the icon painted, she contacted iconographer Paul Tikhomirov, himself a Russian immigrant, to see if he was interested in her project. Tikhomirov's response was, "This icon will be

---

1 The desire of many Russian Christians for the canonization of Tsar Nicholas and his family did not stem from a belief that their personal lives were blameless, although from historical accounts and the family's own letters it is obvious that they were Christians of great integrity. The widespread desire for the family's canonization is based on the fact that Tsar Nicholas and his family were murdered as a result of his position as the sacramentally anointed Orthodox monarch of Russia. In August of 2000 they were canonized by the Russian Orthodox Church as "Passion-Bearers," a designation unique to Orthodox Christianity, which carries the connotation of their both bearing the passion of their murderers and sharing in the passion of Christ. (For further discussion on the role of an anointed monarch and the Royal Family's position as passion-bearers, see "*A Gathered Radiance: The Life of Alexandra Romanov, Russia's Last Empress*" by Nun Nectaria McLees, Valaam Society of America, 1992.)

Opposite: The myrrh-streaming icon of Tsar Nicholas II.

radiant!" They decided to depict Tsar Nicholas in coronation robes, with St. Nicholas, his patron saint, and St. Job, on whose feast the Tsar was born, in the upper right and left hand corners. Below the figures would be printed in Russian, "This Holy Icon is for the Canonization of the Tsar-Martyr in Russia." Ija received the finished icon on May 12, 1996 and then traveled to Texas, where it was blessed by ROCOR Bishop Constantine (Yesensky), an old family friend. The icon, however, was not intended solely for family veneration. Ija and her husband, Harvey Schmit, had already arranged to have paper copies of the icon printed to commemorate the one-hundredth anniversary of the coronation of Tsar Nicholas II (May 14/27, 1896). The distribution of the icons, printed in three sizes, was handled by Ija's own non-profit organization, the Society Honoring Russian Nobility, and income from the icons sold in the West purchased food and medicine for needy pensioners and orphans in Russia. A fourth, smaller version of the icon was printed by the thousands and given away in Russia without charge.

Forty-four thousand copies of the icon were printed, most of which were blessed by Archimandrite Anastasy Sagarski at the Society's annual meeting on September 28, 1996. Several thousand more icons were blessed two days later by Abbot Herman (Podmoshensky), Ija Schmit's brother. Father Herman further promoted the icon by reproducing it on the cover of his popular Russian- language journal "Russky Palomnik," (Russian Pilgrim), which is widely read throughout Russia. As word of the icon spread, Christians from Russia, Ukraine, Belarus, and even Serbia, began writing and requesting copies. The Society has met all these requests and distributed more than twenty thousand icons in Russia alone.

On a visit to Russia in late 1996, Abbot Herman presented a number of prints to Fr. Juvenaly, the priest at the St. Nicholas Almshouse in Ryazan. On March 2/15, 1998 (the anniversary of Tsar Nicholas' abdication and the miraculous appearance of the Reigning Icon of the Mother of God[2]) Fr. Juvenaly blessed Dr. Oleg Belchenko with one of the prints, which the

2 The Reigning ("Derzhavnaya") Icon of the Mother of God was found on March 2/15, 1917, in the storeroom of a church in the village of Kolomenskoe (now part of Moscow proper) by an old woman who had been told in a dream where to find it. The icon depicts the Lord of Sabaoth at the center top, and the Mother of God as the central figure seated on a throne with the crown of the Russian tsars on her head. In one hand she holds a scepter and in the other, an orb. The Infant Christ Child is seated on her knees. This royal image of the Mother of God was discovered on the day of the abdication of Tsar Nicholas II and is called the Reigning Icon of the Mother of God. She is considered by many Orthodox to have assumed the royal authority of the tsars over Russia following the abdication. The icon was hidden during the Communist era, and much sought after by Party officials who were aware of its symbolic value and wanted it destroyed. It is now in a church in Kolomenskoe Park, not far from the original church where it was found.

doctor took with him back to Moscow. The paper icon had been given to him in a glass-fronted, three-dimensional wooden a *kiot* (icon case) and Dr. Belchenko set it in a prominent place in his Moscow apartment.

On September 5, Dr. Belchenko noticed that a red spot had appeared over the right eyelid of the Tsar. The following day a second red spot appeared over the left eye. Dr. Belchenko first compared the icon with a smaller print to male sure that he had not simply overlooked the distinctive marks. The smaller icon did not match. Dr. Belchenko then called the Sretensky Monastery of the Meeting of the Lord to ask what he should do. The monks asked him to bring the icon of Tsar Nicholas to the monastery the following morning. Dr. Belchenko arrived early and stood through the liturgy holding the icon in a plastic bag at his side.

At the end of the liturgy a moleben and blessing of the waters was held. The officiating priest recognized Dr. Belchenko, and knowing that he had come with the icon, had the choir sing a troparion for Tsar-Martyr Nicholas. Following the troparion, Dr. Belchenko noticed one of the parishioners staring at him. Finally, the man approached and asked, "What is that fragrance?" Dr. Belchenko replied: "You are probably smelling incense. I am sorry, I can't smell anything myself because I have a cold." The man persisted: "No. I tell you, the fragrance is coming from somewhere around you and the smell is much more refined than incense." Dr. Belchenko replied impatiently, "You should be ashamed of talking such nonsense while the service is going on!" The man moved away embarrassed, but within a few moments other worshippers filtered over, curious about the fragrance and asking what was in the package. "Nothing, only an icon," he replied. "Show it to us." As Dr. Belchenko opened the package and took out the icon, the remarkable scent filled the church.

The icon of Tsar Nicholas II was displayed for veneration in the monastery church for three weeks. After Dr. Belchenko took it home, the fragrance continued to a lesser degree, and as word began to spread, Muscovites increasingly asked to come to his apartment to venerate the icon. Dr. Belchenko felt that his home was too small to accommodate many visitors, so he asked an Orthodox friend, Alla Dyakova, to keep the icon in her flat, where those who wished could venerate it. When asked how he was able relinquish such a treasure, Dr. Belchenko answered, "The icon is not mine. It belongs to all Russians."

On October 19, Alla Dyakova and Fr. Peter Vlashchenko, a married priest

Air procession with icon to bless St. Petersburg Region, 1999.

150-kilometer procession with icon of Reigning Mother of God and myrrh-streaming icon of Tsar Nicholas II, 1999.

from the Ivanovo region, took the icon to Elder Kirill of St. Sergius Lavra, who was in Peredelkino, outside Moscow. Elder Kirill venerated the icon and blessed Fr. Peter and Alla with the words, "Go. Take the icon to whomever asks for it."

On November 1, the icon was brought to the Martha-Mary Convent in Moscow, founded by Grand Duchess Elizabeth Feodorovna, the sister-inlaw of Tsar Nicholas and herself a new-martyr. The day not only marked the birthday of Elizabeth, but the anniversary of Tsar Nicholas' assuming the throne at his father's death in 1894. The icon of Tsar Nicholas was placed on the analogion next to an icon of Grand Duchess Elizabeth. Throughout the Divine Liturgy the icon of the tsar poured forth waves of fragrance, filling the chapel.

On November 7, 1998, the anniversary of the Bolshevik revolution, Alla called the author to say that myrrh had begun flowing down the glass of the icon case. In the upper right-hand corner of the kiot three streams were trickling downward – not straight down, but making their way toward the face of the tsar. A forth stream ran straight to the bottom. On the left side, two parallel streams sped down the glass with such abundance that a saucer was placed under the case to catch the myrrh. I soon joined the small group that had assembled at Alla's apartment: Hieromonk Longinus and Hierodeacon Januarius from Solovki Monastery, Dr. Belchenko, Margarita Degtyareva, and Alla herself. When I arrived, Fr. Longinus was praying in front of the icon, and as he wiped away the myrrh that was still on the case, it immediately reappeared. I felt strongly that this was a response to the prayers of Orthodox Christians everywhere who love the Royal Family. The myrrh flowed for over four hours.

This was only the beginning. Since the fall of 1998, the twelve-by-fifteen inch icon print has streamed myrrh frequently. The myrrh does not appear on the paper icon, however. It generally forms on the top of glass, either as small beads, or flowing down in rivulets. A few times it has appeared under the glass.

Word spread as the icon of Tsar Nicholas continued streaming myrrh, and the patriarch's office blessed the icon to be placed in the seventeenth-century Church of the Ascension on Gorokhovoye Field, near the Kursk train station. The patriarch's office permitted pannikhidas (services for the departed) to be served in front of the icon, but not molebens (services to saints) as the tsar and his family were not yet officially canonized in Russia. (This directive seems to have been quietly remanded, or was perhaps not fully published, as molebens were spontaneously served almost everywhere. As one priest succinctly explained, "It is a miracle-working icon. Molebens are always served in front of miracle-working icons, never pannikhidas.") The icon remained in the Church of the Ascension from November 14 to February 27, more than three months. A daily diary was kept of the icon's changes, and according to Fr. Vassily Golovanov, the church's priest, the icon gushed myrrh almost every third day. He reported that the fragrance and the myrrh often increased noticeably after services for the Royal Family, particularly on dates associated with the Romanovs. Throughout the winter and spring of 1999, the icon was venerated by thousands of Muscovites, including Olga Nikolaevna Kulikovsky-Romanov, wife of the late Tikhon Nikolaevich Kulikovsky-Romanov (nephew of Tsar Nicholas by the tsar's sister, Grand Duchess Olga Alexandrovna.)

The icon was later taken to many other Moscow churches. One pilgrim recalls, "I saw the icon in August of 1999, the week that it was at the Church of the Dormition on Uspensky Pereulok. There wasn't any myrrh that day, but the icon was giving off an otherworldly fragrance like that of saints' relics. I have honored the tsar and his family for years, and read much about their lives, but here, in front of this icon, I was awestruck. I felt that the entire family was there invisibly, their presence more real than that of the people around me. I was deeply humbled and prayed for a long time."

Ivan Gerasimov, a comparative linguist, recounts: "When the icon came to our church, several of the priests, the two choirs, and many parishioners were lined up to greet it. A moleben was served and afterward the choirs, standing on either side of the icon sang "God Save the Tsar." It was incredible. Everyone was in tears. As we stood in line to venerate the icon, I felt as if I had gone back a century, and was waiting to greet the tsar himself. His presence was so real that I suddenly understood, in an instant, all that we have lost."

On days particularly associated with the Royal Family, such as the anniversary of their deaths, or on their namesdays and birthdays, the icon gives off more myrrh, once even rushing down the glass so copiously that it blocked out the view of the paper print. This icon of Tsar-Martyr Nicholas has become a symbol of repentance for thousands of Russians who mourn the regicide of the tsar and his family, and honor them as passion-bearers. Thousands of Orthodox Christians, including hundreds of priests and sev-

Dr. Belechenko holding icon of Tsar Nicholas II, and Fr. Peter Vlashchenko with icon of the Virgin.

Venerating the myrrh-streaming icon of Tsar Nicholas II. Left to right: Priest of the Church of the Ascension on Gorokhovoye Field; Dr. Oleg Belchenko; Olga Nikolaevna Kulikovsky-Romanov (wife of Tikhon Kulikovsky-Romanov, the nephew of Tsar Nicholas II). November, 1998.

eral Russian bishops have venerated the icon, including Archbishop Micah of Yaroslavl and Rostov, Archbishop Ambrose of Ivanovo and Metropolitan Agathangel of Odessa, all of whom received it into their churches and conducted services before it.

The myrrh-streaming icon print of Tsar Nicholas soon became world news. Elena Yugina, a reporter with ITAR-TASS, the Russian news agency, announced that Patriarch Alexis II had given permission for international film crews to cover the story. A Swiss television crew, as well as journalists from CNN, the Associated Press, the Reuters News Agency and a major Spanish paper came to film the icon at the church in Gorokhovoye Field. Accounts appeared in every major Russian newspaper and many magazines. A Russian documentary, "The Return," has been made about the icon, and is currently available in Moscow. A second documentary by Orthodox filmmaker Larissa Tyabus, featuring scenes from services and processions with the icon, will be released in the summer of 2000.

The Associated Press was the first to print an official statement from the Russian Patriarchate concerning the icon. Metropolitan Kirill (Gundyaev) of Smolensk, who heads the Office of External Church Relations stated, "This occurrence, as an indication of God's grace, will be carefully studied and reviewed by the Synodal Commission on the Canonization of Saints to determine whether it is of divine origin." He added that the question of glorification of the Royal Family would be decided at a local council of the Russian Orthodox Church to be held in the year 2000.

The icon has not always remained in Moscow. Along with shorter residences in many Moscow churches, it has been taken to distant parts of Russia. From July 12-17, 1999 the icon was carried 150 kilometers (93 miles) on foot in a procession from St. Tikhon of Lukh Monastery in the Ivanovo diocese to Ipatiev Monastery in Kostroma—the monastery where the first Romanov was chosen as tsar. Twenty-five men, thirty-seven women and five children began the procession, while dozens of others joined it for a few hours or even days enroute. Fourteen clergymen from the Ivanovo and Kostroma regions also walked with the icon. The icon was carried from town to town, and people poured into the streets – old and young lining up behind one another on their knees as the icon was carried past.

Bystanders also knelt in the center of the road so that the icon could be carried over their heads as a blessing. Elderly women limped painfully out to the procession route to venerate the icon. Groups of children ran to keep ahead as the procession moved through the streets, that they might watch it pass again and again. Everywhere the scenes were repeated. One priest who accompanied the icon remarked, "Although the Royal Martyrs have not yet been officially canonized by the hierarchs of the Russian Orthodox Church, the people are not waiting for such a proclamation. Their veneration pours forth freely, wherever the icon of Tsar-Martyr Nicholas appears."

Alla Dyakova, one of the participants recalls, "Many people joined the procession along the way and walked with us for a day or two; one woman carried a nursing baby in her arms. Two blind men from St. Petersburg were with us for the entire five days, and one of them was also missing a foot, so he hobbled the whole distance on crutches. Five children walked the one hundred fifty kilometers without complaint. In the countryside, local people came out to meet us. They venerated the myrrh-streaming icon of the Tsar with tears in their eyes and gave us *piroshki*, pickles, tomatoes, bread... whatever they had to eat."

In Ivanovo, the icon was brought in procession to the home chapel of Archbishop Ambrose of Ivanovo where services were held. Myrrh gushed from the icon in seven streams, and during the services the glass was entirely covered with myrrh. The archbishop placed a copy of the icon against the glass, and his paper copy, too, began to give off myrrh. The following day, Archbishop Ambrose and his clergy received the icon of the tsar, along with his own myrrh-streaming copy, at Transfiguration Cathedral in Ivanovo. Throughout the entire service myrrh gushed from both icons.

On the 16th of July 1999, the procession continued to the women's Monastery of the Annunciation in Kostroma, where another wonderworking icon traditionally associated with the Romanov family is enshrined. It was with this icon, the Feodorov Mother of God, that Nun Martha blessed her seventeen- year-old son, Michael Feodorovich Romanov, to become the Russian tsar, in 1613, thus founding the Romanov dynasty.[3] Now, 386 years later, the last Russian tsar entered the church once again, in the form of his myrrh-streaming icon. As the icon of the tsar was touched to the Feodorov Mother of God, a broad band of myrrh formed at the top of the glass and eight thick lines streamed down the front.

---

3 The Feodorovskaya Icon of the Mother of God is associated with the Holy Great-Martyr Theodore (Feodor) Stratelates, a fourth-century soldier martyred for Christ. St. Theodore, holding this icon, appeared several times to Russian Christians following the Tartar invasions. The original Feodorovskaya Icon of the Mother of God is of Byzantine origin and is located in the women's Monastery of the Annunciation in Kostroma.

On the morning of July 17 (the anniversary of the Royal Family's murder in 1918 at the Ipatiev House in Ekaterinburg) the icon arrived at the Ipatiev Monastery in Kostroma. As soon as the icon was placed on the analogion in the main cathedral, myrrh began flowing more profusely than ever. This time there were eleven streams and the entire glass was covered with the thick fragrant liquid. Throughout the entire service the icon gave off a strong, otherworldly fragrance. Alla Dyakova continues:

"It is impossible to put into words all that we felt here...we had all come together – people from different regions, yet bound together in our love for the tsar. That is how I would put it. We were bonded in love. Everyone became so close during the procession that we were like a family. As time went on, we began to hope the day would never arrive when the procession would be over and we would have to leave each other. When we reached Ipatiev Monastery, all eighty-six of us gave confession and partook of Holy Communion. At confession we all confessed our personal repentance for the act of regicide committed against the tsar and his family. How can I put this into words? It was a feeling of deep sorrow for everything that had happened, and no one was left unmoved. Yet we also shed tears of joy at the abundance of God's mercy when we saw the extraordinary amount of myrrh that gushed from the Icon of the Tsar-Martyr that day."

At the end of summer, September 3-14, 1999, the icon was taken to St. Petersburg for veneration in the city's churches. The resident clergy often awaited the icon's arrival holding burning candles and dressed in red vestments – the traditional color for martyrs. During the icon's reception at the Optina Pustyn metochion in St. Petersburg, over nine thousand people passed through the doors in one day. On September 13, the icon was received at the Feodorovsky Cathedral in Tsarskoe Selo, where a copy of the Feodorov Icon of the Mother of God is enshrined and where Tsar Nicholas II and his family worshipped.[4] Ten thousand pilgrims came from St. Petersburg and surrounding areas to venerate.

4 Feodorovsky Cathedral in Tsarskoe Selo was erected between 1909 and 1912 by Tsar Nicholas II outside the gates of the Alexander Palace in honor of the Feodorovskaya Icon of the Mother of God, an icon traditionally associated with the Romanov Dynasty. As noted above, the original Feodorov Icon is in Kostroma.

One of the pilgrims recounts, "When we were at Tsarskoe Selo we had services at the Royal Family's church – I remember the priest there showing me the column where the tsar and his family stood during services. I stayed right next to the same column and thought to myself, "I can't believe I am actually standing in the very place where the royal family used to stand." I wept through the entire service."

In Kronstadt, the naval town next to St. Petersburg, the icon was carried to the home of St. John of Kronstadt, who was himself a wonder-worker. When the procession stopped on the street in front of the house, the inside of the glass cover filled with myrrh, obliterating the view of the icon, and taking on the image – in myrrh – of the icon itself. The icon of Tsar Nicholas was then taken up in a helicopter and an attending priest used it to bless the city of St. Petersburg, where it had been so warmly received.

Not everyone greeted the icon with the same enthusiasm, however. Soon after arrangements were made to bring the icon to St. Petersburg, phone calls went out from the diocesan office of Metropolitan Vladimir of St. Petersburg to the three churches where it was to be received, telling them not to accept it. Two of the churches did not receive the icon, but twelve others did. The protopriest of the third forewarned church received the icon and was removed from his position two months later, on ostensibly unrelated grounds.

The most wide-spread attempt to bring the icon to the attention of the Russian people was the organization of an "Air Procession" by Sergei Matveyev, the editor-in-chief of the Orthodox magazine Russky Vestnik and Andrei Melanovich, from the publishing department of Sretensky Monastery. With the blessings of Patriarch Alexis II and Elder Nicholas (Guryanov) of Zalit Island near Pskov, a plane containing copies of miraculous icons (the copies often being wonder-working themselves), as well as other original icons set with the relics of saints, flew to the four corners of Russia. The flight's mission was to bring these spiritual treasures to Orthodox Christians who had never before been able to venerate them. Taking off from Moscow on the morning of June 14, 1999, the flight covered 15,500 miles (25,000 km). It was fortythree hours in the air.

Along with the myrrh-streaming icon of Tsar Nicholas, the walls and the tables of the plane were covered with more than sixty original icons and hundreds of paper prints. There was also a cross from Optina Monastery containing relics of the Optina elders, and holy oil from lampadas and icons on Mt. Athos. At the moment of take-off, the icon of Tsar Nicholas began giving forth the same otherworldly fragrance that had characterized it throughout the year. The flight's first direction was southward, over Minsk and Kiev, between Simferopol and Sebastopol, towards Yalta and Mineralniye Vodi. From Ukraine and the Crimea the planeload of icons flew to Astrakhan, the first scheduled landing. As the attendants prepared to open the doors to pilgrims who had arrived to venerate, they noticed that the lower half of the glass covering the tsar's icon was beaded with small drops of fragrant myrrh.

After Astrakhan the plane turned northeasterly, flying over Volgograd and Saratov, and landing in Novosibirsk (Novonikolaevsk), Siberia. After Novosibirsk came Khabarovsk, then deeper into Siberia, and over Sakhalin Island on the edge of the Russian Far East. Finally they arrived at the peninsula of Kamchatka on the Bering Sea, where they again landed and served a moleben to the Reigning Mother of God. The next stop was Anadyr on Chukotka Peninsula, the easternmost point of Russia. Although the local churches had been notified of their coming, these isolated Christians are so unaccustomed to such spiritual largesse that they met the plane with reserve, afraid that the flight was a ruse by foreign Baptist missionaries to attract an audience. Once the town's leaders and local clergy were reassured, over a hundred Orthodox faithful came to venerate the icon. Holding the myrhh-streaming icon, Ivonovo's Fr. Peter Vlashchenko addressed the crowd. They listened attentively to its history, and as he finished with, "God willing, there will once again come a time in Russia when we will have a tsar," a voice spoke up from the midst of the crowd. "Yes, it is time to get our house in order!"

From Anadyr, the procession flew to Khatanga in north central Siberia, where they landed on the 18th of June. Father Peter recalled, "We were greeted at the airport by the local authorities and a priest, Fr. Daniel. A television crew filmed the event. Throughout the day fifty to sixty people came to venerate the icon. We gave copies of the icon to almost everyone. I particularly remember one woman who venerated the icons with deep reverence and tears, totally unmindful of the TV cameras and those standing near her."

Flying over Pskov-Pechury, the site of the famous Pskov Caves Monastery, the plane landed in Archangelsk where an akathist was sung to St. Nilus of

Sora. It then flew over Murmansk, Solovki Monastery in the White Sea, and Valaam Monastery on Lake Ladoga, until it finally turned back towards Moscow.

Many Orthodox Christians believe that their prayers have been answered by God through the intercession of the tsar and his family. One of these is Alexander Vytegov, who at age eighty-seven was healed of blindness in front of the myrrh-streaming icon of Tsar Martyr Nicholas II.

In 1984, Alexander was diagnosed with an eye disease in which cells in the center of the retina begin to die off. Doctors could do nothing to help him, and within a few years his correctable vision was reduced to less than thirty percent. Alexander had been an atheist for many decades and had habitually referred to Tsar Nicholas as "Bloody Nicholas," a period of his life that he now regrets. In his early seventies, he began reading a borrowed bible to round out his grasp of history. "I was caught up in it, and finally started to understand." After obtaining his own copy of the Gospels, Alexander was further drawn to Christ and the Church. A few years later, he suffered a major heart attack, underwent emergency surgery and recovered. Convinced that he had been saved through the intercession of the Mother of God, Alexander became a practicing Orthodox Christian. Then, in 1999 he heard Fr. Alexander Shargunov speaking on Radio Radonezh about people who had been healed through the intercession of the Tsar-Martyr. Learning that the myrrh-streaming icon was in the Church of the Holy Trinity on Khokhlovsky Lane in Moscow, he went there on June 2 to attend a moleben. After the service, Alexander made his way to the priest, Fr. Alexy Uminsky, asking to be healed of his blindness. Fr. Alexy answered, "If you want to be healed, pray to Tsar-Martyr Nicholas with me. Alexander describes what happened next:

> Father Alexy led me over to the icon of Tsar-Martyr Nicholas and placed my face right on the icon, holding my head down with his hand. Then he covered my face with a towel that had myrrh on it from the icon and began to pray. I don't know what prayer he recited, because my hearing is poor. Then he raised my head and covered my face with the towel containing the myrrh and pressed the towel to my eyes with his fingers three times, while saying another prayer. A few days later I had to write something. It was June 9th.

Before then I had to write from memory, because I couldn't see the lines. I had to write letter by letter, and if I got distracted, I never knew which letter to write next... but then, my Lord – I still can't believe it – I could see! I could see everything! I could see the lines, and the letters. I can't believe it even now, but I really do see. After this healing I know once and for all that the tsar truly prays for those who love him and the Lord helps people through his prayers. The Lord is long-suffering. How long He waited for me – and in the end, He didn't reject me."

Amen. ✛

SAINTS ALIVE!

(or "The Bits the Hagiographers Left Out")

Sts. Basil and Gregory: Survivors of a Miserable Wreck

There are only a few Orthodox saints to whom the church has granted the title, "the Great": Athanasius of Alexandria, Anthony, Macarius and Euthymius of the Egyptian Thebaid, and Basil of Cappadocia. As both the founder of organized cenobitic monasticism in the West, and the ascetic

Photo: The Three Holy Hierarchs: Sts. Basil, John Chrysostom, and Gregory the Theologian.

warrior-bishop who threw his tempered intellect into battle against the Arians, Basil's title fits him well. His name fits him even better. He stands in Orthodox tradition as a king: noble, principled and imperious.

It was in his retreat at Ibora, near Cappadocia (in modern-day Turkey) that the young Basil forged his famous monastic rule. Even today there are distinct traces of the Basilian rule threaded through Greek and Slavic monasticism, and Basil inscribed his legacy in two versions: the Shorter Rule, and the Longer. Ibora was a wild and mountainous spot on the edge of Asia Minor and Basil lived there, first with Gregory Nazianzen (St. Gregory the Theologian) and then with a growing number of disciples, including, for a time, his own brothers Peter and Gregory (of Nyssa). In the rule he recommended nothing he had not done himself. Physical labor included hauling manure, chopping firewood, and dressing the rough stones to be used for building. Worship services were long and fervent, food was poor, discipline exact – and Basil, with his iron temperament, gloried in it.

Years later, in a letter warm with affection and good humor, Gregory Nazianzen reminded Basil of their sojourn at Ibora, and we read with delight his account of an early rescue of the young ascetics:

> Your roofless and doorless hut, your fireless and smokeless hearth, your walls dried by fire, that we may not be hit by the drops of mud, condemned like Tantalus thirsting in the midst of waters, and that pitiable feast with nothing to eat, to which we were invited from Cappadocia, not as to a Lotus-eater's poverty, but to a table of Alcinous – we young and miserable survivors of a wreck. For I remember those loaves and the broth (so it was called), yes, and I shall remember them too, and my poor teeth that slipped on your hunks of bread, and then braced themselves up, and pulled themselves as it were out of mud. You yourself will raise these things to a higher strain of tragedy, having learnt to talk big through your own sufferings... for if we had not been quickly delivered by that great supporter of the poor – I mean your mother – who appeared opportunely like a harbour to men tossed by a storm, we should long ago have been dead, rather pitied than admired for our faith in Pontus...[1] ✦

1 Letters of St. Gregory Nazianzen, Division II, Letter 5, Eerdman's Post-Nicene Fathers.

TALKS WITH ORTHODOX CHRISTIANS

My Road to Emmaus

There are times in our lives when – like the two disciples on the *Road to Emmaus* – we find ourselves in situations where our eyes are opened to Christ's presence. We asked Orthodox believers to share with us some instances that affected their lives and helped to set them on their spiritual search.

Ludmilla Nikolaevna, 55, Kiev, Ukraine

There were three children in my family–myself, a younger sister and a younger brother. Our father died early on and our mother, who still lives with me, is totally blind. I never married. I guess I had too many worries helping my mother and just trying to survive. My sister was married young and had a daughter, but she later divorced and became very sad. We tried our best to help her through this period, but she fell into deeper and deeper depression. She worked as a waitress in a hotel restaurant, but the pay never seemed to be enough. Several years ago she jumped off the balcony and fell seven stories to her death. We were all in shock.

We never heard about God when we were growing up. We only heard about some kind of socialist-style paradise that was always just around the corner. I met an Orthodox believer once who asked me how I could deal with all these things in my life without faith in God, seeing that there had to be more meaning to life than just living and dying. I had never given it any thought; it was all so foreign to me. But after my sister's death, I experienced a terrible urgency to make sense of everything that had occurred. That's the moment my spiritual life began. I now go to church and thank God for the little light I do see in my life.

Andrei Valerievich, 21, Ivanovo

Last year I received an honorable discharge after serving in the Army. My time spent there started out as a nightmare. I worked with an Army construction crew on projects in Moscow, and on our work crew were two soldiers who hazed all the new recruits. No one had any money to buy anything and these soldiers would force two of us recruits to walk about the streets all day begging for money. Everything we received had to be turned over to them. In the beginning we only had to collect a bit, but the amount we had to bring back grew each day and if we failed to meet our quota, we were beaten up. The other soldier on the work crew told our captain of these threats. He was already aware of the situation, and was maybe even taking part of the money himself because the two soldiers were told who had reported them. They beat the guy up so badly he had to be hospitalized and not a thing was done about it. It was an "accident." One day, I was in despair. It was winter in Moscow and my boots were soaking wet from the slush. I was freezing cold but I had to endure it or be beaten.

Then one day I went up to a man to ask him for money. It turned out he was an Orthodox believer. He spoke to me about faith, invited me in for something to eat and a hot cup of tea and allowed me to call my mother, whom I hadn't seen for six months. All I can remember is crying a lot. It was like I was given new life that day. This person then helped me get a transfer to another battalion where things became much better for me. I was baptized as a young boy, but it was only after this experience that I really began wearing a cross. That was when I became a believer.

Ekaterina Lavrentievna, 57, Kishinev (Moldavia)

I am 57 years old. All my life I've lived in Kishinev. My father was a good man, but had no faith in God and dealt with his emptiness by drinking. My mother raised five children in very difficult circumstances and two of whom died early in life. I was married when I was seventeen and had a son whom I secretly had baptized at an early age.

God was something we never learned about in the Soviet years. No one ever told us that God was real. How to explain this? I had no logical proof, but somehow I knew He was real. I think it was my grandmother's quiet faith that inspired me. She always made the sign of the cross over us whenever we went out. At first it seemed like just a motion of her hands, but a warm feeling always stayed with me from that.

Maria Vladimirovna, 32, Smolensk

I remember the day and everything that happened afterwards very well. It was in the spring, eleven years ago – in May, to be exact. I lived in Moscow at the time and was returning home from Smolensk, where my four-year-old daughter Anastasia and I had been visiting my parents. When we arrived home, my husband Vadim was not there, but he arrived shortly after we finished having breakfast. As soon as he looked at me, I knew right away that something was bothering him and that he wanted to talk. As soon as we were alone, Vadim told me that he was planning to leave me. I was in shock. Even though we had often had arguments and our family life was not always easy, I wasn't ready for this. Questions flooded my mind: How will I live? Where? What about our daughter?

My husband left. I was now alone. It was a beautiful, clear, sunny spring day outside – and I was completely alone with an inconsolable pain inside me. I remember several days at home, going out only once or twice to do some shopping. Thoughts and hurt filled my head.

One evening soon after I turned on the television and watched a documentary on the life of Anastasia Tsvetaeva (the sister of the famous poetess, Marina Tsvetaeva). She was already an old woman, but kind and full of life. I remember her sitting on a park bench and sharing some of her life and memories. But then, she suddenly spoke of how each year she would visit a wonderful monastery with a healing spring and how each winter she would bathe in this water and feel absolutely renewed. Her story interested me very much, perhaps because it helped me forget my own pain a little. Later, I tried hard but couldn't recall the name of the monastery she was speaking of. All I remembered was that it was in Estonia. Then I went to sleep.

I awoke the next morning to a beautiful, sunny day. The thought flashed in my mind that somehow I had to find this monastery. I made up my mind to do this, and a great burden seemed to fall from my shoulders, as if this was the answer! (At the time I didn't realize that this was really my Salvation; not just salvation in one particular situation.) I felt so much better that I fell back asleep.

On another beautiful, sunny day in May, I left for Tallin, the capital of Estonia – which at that time was still a part of the Soviet Union. I had no idea where the monastery was located or even what it was called, but somehow I knew I would find it. Just as soon as the train had crossed over into Estonia a fellow passenger in my compartment said: "Not far from here is a wonderful women's monastery. And how the nuns there can sing!" I tried hard to remember the name of the station we had just passed. I thought it was Johvi.

After arriving in Tallin the next morning, I immediately went to the bus station where I bought a ticket to Johvi. Once in Johvi, I was told I had to go just a bit farther to a place called Kuremäe where I would find the famous Pühtitsa Monastery. I spent three weeks there and didn't want to leave. Everyone was so nice to me. It was as if they knew I was having a hard time in my life and did everything they could to be kind to me.

I was convinced that I would be coming here often, but things turned out quite differently. An old pilgrim visiting Pühtitsa told me about another monastery and its spiritual father. At the time I paid very little attention to his words, but two months after returning home to my parents and daughter, I felt a strong desire to return once again to Pühtitsa. I thought that it would be a good idea to stop along the way and pay a visit to the monastery that the pilgrim had spoken to me about, Rizhskaya Pustyn, where I met Archimandrite Peter, the priest who was to become my spiritual father and open up spiritual life to me.

Vladimir Romanovich, 26, Moscow

When I was a child I spent each summer in the country with my grand parents. They were Baptists and would always take me along with them to church on Sunday. There for the first time I heard of God, the Bible and Jesus Christ. At home I loved to play "church" with my grandparents – I would read the Bible out loud, interrupting my reading with amusing remarks like: "Don't fall asleep, brother!," something which I had heard when I was at their church. My grandparents gladly played along with me, considering such a naive and child-like acceptance of their faith as something quite positive. Once my uncle, who was living with my grandmother in the same village, asked me: "Don't tell me you believe all of grandmother's fairy tales? Don't you know that cosmonauts flew into space and didn't see God there?" I don't remember whether my faith was really shaken at the time; I only remember that I wasn't able to give him an answer.

Then there was the time when the Commission from our local Public Education Department came to our first-grade class and asked the seven-year-olds whether any of us believed in God. I got scared and kept quiet, remembering the story about the cosmonauts. Then someone from the Commission asked another question: "Do your parents or any of your relatives believe in God?" This time my hand shot up into the air. I was an honest child, who had always been taught to tell the truth. After I answered, "Yes, my grandmother believes in God," an awkward silence hung over the classroom. The teacher tried to remedy the situation, assuring the members of the Commission that I had gotten something mixed up. That evening she phoned my home and spoke with my mother for a long time, saying that she had never expected such a thing from me – such an excellent and exemplary pupil. After her talk with my parents I began to suspect that something was wrong in the world of adults if they forced you to lie while teaching you to be honest.

After this experience, my parents, who until then hadn't minded my going to church with my grandparents, forbade my grandmother to take me with her. Then came the Pioneer gatherings of my childhood, the Komsomol meetings of my youth, and perestroika, with its attempt to change the world. I began to forget about God, and was keen on reading books about spies and revolutionaries. But the euphoria over glasnost and perestroika quickly subsided and I saw once again that the world of adults (I myself had just finished school) was as false as before. They spoke of perestroika, democracy and freedom, but these were only words. Once I was even called to appear before the Local Committee of the Komsomol for having used the Biblical metaphor about not pouring new wine into old wineskins at a local meeting of Komsomol activists and Party bosses. They reprimanded me for talking about the "opium of the people..."

At that time I became interested in philosophy and wanted to enter the Philosophy Department at the University of the Urals. In order to acquaint ourselves with university life, some friends and I traveled to Sverdlovsk (now called Ekaterinburg), where we spent a few days. We went to lectures, spoke with students, ate in the student cafeterias, and so forth. I became deeply disenchanted with the philosophy majors, however, because they were engaged in everything but philosophy, which, as far as I was concerned, was supposed to attempt to answer the question about the meaning of life. At that time the main criteria for philosophy majors at the University of the Urals was participation in the Urals People's Political Front. I understood then that I wouldn't be entering this university.

Soon my older friend and teacher, with whom I read and discussed philosophical books, began to talk to me about Christianity. Under his influence I began to study the Bible again, reading one that my grandmother had given me as a gift. I began to try to find in life that which I called "moral purity in the ideal." Reading the Bible, I understood that if that moral purity I was seeking really existed on earth, then it had to be Christianity. All of this took place rather smoothly, without any particular experiences or events. My reasoning was more or less this: if there is no God, I won't lose anything by living according to Christian laws; but if He does exist, I will acquire something that I will never be able to receive anywhere else.

I was still far from Orthodoxy at that time; moreover, my Baptist background had inculcated in me a rather critical attitude towards fasting, priests and icons. Even all the Christian literature that I had read up until then was not in the least Orthodox. They were either Protestant books or good classical works on religion. Leo Tolstoy's *Confession* made a very strong impression on me, as did Francois Mauriac's *Life of Christ*, I continue to find highly interesting and useful. I came to Orthodoxy quietly, without any mental anguish.

Then a friend of mine who was getting married asked me if I would be a witness. Seeing that I had been baptized Orthodox as a child, I was only required to wear a cross around my neck. I put it on, and from that moment I have never taken off that cross. It just seemed necessary to keep wearing it. There was nothing mystical about the feeling, I can't even call it a deeply thought out step. I simply decided that, "I will be with the cross."

It was later, after I entered the institute, that I began going to church: I wore a cross, considered myself Orthodox, and went to church. In addition to attending church on Sundays, I began reading the new Orthodox literature that was beginning to appear, and spent more and more time in church. The spiritual treasure of Orthodoxy began to open itself up to me. It was at this time, also, that I began experiencing my first serious difficulties and temptations.

I cannot say that everything is easy and that I never have had second thoughts about the rightness of my decision. But when I look back on the past, I see a very deep meaning in this simple path which I have described. I see how my life continues to be tranformed, filled with meaning, and I joyfully say: "Thank God that this world has been opened up to me, this treasure has been given to me so freely." Simply because I once wore a cross. ✦

See what milestones you may have missed along the road.

BACK ISSUES: $11.95 each (includes shipping/handling) for U.S.

TO SUBSCRIBE/ORDER BY MAIL:
Please send check or money order to:
Road to Emmaus, P.O. Box 16021, Portland, Oregon, 97292-0021

TO SUBSCRIBE/ORDER ONLINE:
www.roadtoemmaus.net

INTERNATIONAL SUBSCRIPTIONS/BACK ISSUE ORDERS:
For international back issue orders or subscriptions, please order by credit card through our website
(or if you prefer to pay by mail, write or call us for personalized payment or shipping options).

CALL US AT: 1-866-783-6628 (M-F, 9:00AM – 8:00PM, PST)

*NOTE: We are unable to take credit card orders over the phone. If you wish to
subscribe by credit card, please do so on our website. Questions/Comments?*

SPRING 2018
ISSUE No. 73

- Freeing the Soul: Reflections on Thirty Years as an Orthodox Confessor

WINTER 2018
ISSUE No. 72

- Orthodoxy in Greater China: Laying the Foundation for an International Orthodox Presence
- Heirs of St. Seraphim's Wonderful Revelation: The Moscow Descendants of Nikolai Motovilov
- The Motoviloffs in America: Tracking our Russian Roots
- As Bright as the Sun: Excerpts from "the Conversation of St. Seraphim and N.A. Motovilov"

SUMMER FALL 2017
ISSUE No. 70-71

- I. Christianity Comes Over the Alps
- II. The Martyrs of the Swiss Alps
- III. Missionary Saints of Switzerland

WINTER SPRING 2017
ISSUE No. 68-69

- Pilgrimage to Lesvos: The Spiritual Treasury of a Greek Island
- Living Faith and Unsung Saints: Memories of a Holy Island
- "To Help Them Safely From the Sea…": The Heroism of Lesvos' Greek Villages
- Orthodoxy in the Urals: Remembering Verkhoturye
- Acquiring Faith: A Siberian Childhood

FALL 2016
ISSUE No. 67

- Living with Lions: The St. Mary of Egypt Animal Sanctuary
- Animals, Man and God: Orthodoxy and the Animal Kingdom
- On the Nature and Souls of Animals
- The Snakes of Markopoulo

SPRING SUMMER 2016
ISSUE No. 65-66

- Saint Innocent of Alaska and Sitka's Russian-American Heritage
- Following the Star: Conversations with Sitka Elders
- Sitka's Cathedral of Archangel Michael: An Historic Russian Church in a Land of Saints
- A Russian Priest in Alta California
- Remembering Saint Innocent
- Russian Church Bells on California's El Camino Real

WINTER 2016
ISSUE No. 64

- Reflecting the Heavenly Jerusalem: Building New Churches with Dignity and Grace
- All Manner of Things Beautiful: Met. Hilarion of Kiev's Sermon on Law and Grace
- A Crown of Beauty in the Hand of the Lord: Patriarch Photios on the Restoration of Hagia Sophia

FALL 2015
ISSUE No. 63

- On Earth as it is in Heaven: Form and Meaning in Orthodox Architecture
- "Mass Transfigured By Light": The Iconic Vision of an Orthodox Church
- "We Cannot Forget That Beauty": Notes on Sources for the Conversion of Rus'

SUMMER 2015
ISSUE No. 62

- Facing Eternity in a Russian Hospice: Sustaining Compassion and Love in the Final Days
- A Peaceful Passing: Negotiating the Hospital and Hospice
- A Simple Grace
- Clothed in White Linen
- Sweet Relief: Greek Burial Rites and Ritual Lamentation

SPRING 2015
ISSUE No. 61

- On the High Road with Scotland's Saints: Six Early Christian Pilgrimage Destinations
- Columba's Children: Life and Community on a Holy Island
- How the Vikings Got Their Comeuppance: "Iona's Revenge"
- New Beginnings: Orthodoxy in Today's Scotland

**WINTER
2015
ISSUE No. 60**

- Chastity and Empathy: Eros, Agape, and the Mystery of the TwoFold Anointing
  An Interview in Three Parts

**FALL
2014
ISSUE No. 59**

- "Kicking the Earth from Under Your Feet": A Russian Scenographer on Seeing Ordinary Things
  in New Ways
- An Actor's Pilgrimage, A Life in Progress
- An Insatiable Desire to Share the Excitement: The Actor as a Young Man

**SUMMER
2014
ISSUE No. 58**

- Orthodoxy in Contemporary Sweden: From Viking-Era Christian Roots to a 21st-century
  Pan-Orthodox Theological Academy
- "Carrying the Tradition": Thoughts on Orthodox Parish Life in Today's Sweden
- A Swedish Princess in Kievan Rus: The Medieval Christian World of St. Anna of Novgorod

**SPRING
2014
ISSUE No. 57**

- A Feeling for Beauty: The Aesthetic Ground of Orthodox Ethics
- St. Theophan the Recluse: How to Love Christ
- Divine Eros in the Counsels of St. Porphyrios the New

**WINTER
2014
ISSUE No. 56**

- His Life in Christ: A Pilgrimage to the Holy Places of St. John of Kronstadt
- An American in Tsarist Russia: Isabel Hapgood's Meeting with St. John of Kronstadt
- In His Own Words: St. John of Kronstadt on Prayer and Warmth of Heart

**FALL
2013
ISSUE No. 55**

- Salvation and the Free Life of the Spirit in the Orthodox Canonical Tradition
- Nadezhda Savova's Bread Houses: Bread-Making as Food, Art, Healing, Prayer, and International
  Community

**SUMMER
2013
ISSUE No. 54**

- An Intimation of the Sacred: The Iconography of Hieromonk Silouan Justiniano
- Beauty as a Double-Edged Sword: Icons, Authenticity, and Reproductions
  I. Beyond Appearances: Classical Techniques and Sacred Painting
  II. The Iconicity of the Icon
- Incarnational Aesthetics

**SPRING
2013
ISSUE No. 53**

- "The Mystery that Moves the World Now Has a Name": How 150,000 Mayans Turned to Orthodoxy
- Ahora y Siempre! A Seminarian's Travels in Orthodox Guatemala
- Popol Vuh: A Mayan Tale of Creation

**WINTER
2013
ISSUE No. 52**

- War, Byzantium, and Military Saints
- The Opposite of War is Not Peace: Healing Trauma in *The Iliad* and in Orthodox Tradition
- Coda: Invoking God in War – Lincoln's Picture of the Second Inaugural
- Defending Russia: Belief and Coming of Age in the Soviet Army

**FALL
2012
ISSUE No. 51**

- Reading Hagiography: How to Engage those Astonishing, Perplexing, Archaic,
  and Stunningly Grace-Filled Saints' Lives
- Byzantine Bride-Shows and the Restoration of Icons: A Tale of Four Iconophile Empresses
- Early Church Writers on Hagiography

SUMMER 2012 ISSUE No. 50
- Turkey and the First Throne of Orthodoxy: A Reconsideration
- Euripides and Puccini under the Ottomans: The Surprising Richness of Greek Girls' Schools in the Late Empire
- The Seal of the Gift of the Holy Spirit: Preparing Chrism at the Ecumenical Patriarchate

SPRING 2012 ISSUE No. 49
- Natural Conception, Natural Birth: The New Hope for Infertility
- The Hospitality of Abraham: Orthodox Ethics and Reproduction
- The Embryo in Orthodox Christian Theology and Tradition
- While as Yet He Was in His Mother's Womb…

WINTER 2012 ISSUE No. 48
- Orphans in Contemporary Russia: The Russian Orphan Opportunity Fund
- Inspiration in The Making
- Orphanages and Philanthropy in Byzantium

FALL 2011 ISSUE No. 47
- A Different Light: Youthful Travelers in Contemporary America
- Death to The World: An Orthodox Punk 'Zine Revived and Revisited
- Death to The World in Print
- Catching Xenophilia: Contagious Hospitality in Orthodox Parishes

SUMMER 2011 ISSUE No. 46
- Early Orthodox in British America
- An Orthodox Christian Fired the First Shot in the American Civil War
- Louis Tikas: 1914 Passion-Bearer of the Colorado Coal Fields
- Remembering Tikas: A Pilgrimage to Loutra

SPRING 2011 ISSUE No. 45
- Croagh Patrick: The Glorious Climb of Ireland's Holy Mountain
- Asenath on the Reek
- The Spirit set in Motion: Revisiting St. Patrick's Mission to Ireland
- Over the White-Capped Sea: Eight Late Antique Irish Poems

WINTER 2011 ISSUE No. 44
- Optina's Second Spring: The Rebirth of a Russian Monastery
- Narrow Escapes of Grace: An Interview with Matusha Agapia (Minchenkova)
- The Orthodox Clock and The Map of The World

FALL 2010 ISSUE No. 43
- Taybeh's Plea For The Last Christians of The Holy Land
- The Marvellous Life of Patriarch Sophronius I, His Company of Saints, and The Fall of Byzantine Jerusalem
- The Holy City of Jerusalem

SUMMER 2010 ISSUE No. 42
- Saint Nectarios of Pentapolis: The Aegina Years
- The Great-grandmother: A Childhood on Aegina
- The Mystery of Holy Language
  - I. Liturgical Languages and Living Tadition
  - II. Coming Home to Church Greek
  - III. Defending Old Languages: Cultures, Discourse, and Heaven

SPRING 2010 ISSUE No. 41
- Coming Into One's Own Among Strangers at Home: German Orthodoxy Rekindled
- Orthodox Roots, Woods, and Water: A Decade of Pilgrimage to Germany and Switzerland
- The Advent of Orthodoxy in The German-Speaking Lands
- Pilgrimage to Eichstätt: Sts. Willibald, Walburga and Wunibald
- The Travels of Willibald: A.D. 721-727

WINTER 2010
ISSUE No. 40
- Stepping Into The Stream: An Interview with Alice C. Linsley
- Holy Wells of Wales
- The Unbroken Tradition: St. Winifred's Well (Ffynnon Wenfrewi) Holywell
- Holy Water and Pseudoscience: Who Needs Experiments on Holy Things?

FALL 2009
ISSUE No. 39
- Souls in Motion: Creativity and Community in a Harlem Workshop
- Dear Julia: Words From Souls
- Where the Cross Divides the Road (Part II)
- Babouscka: A Russian Christmas Story for Children

SUMMER 2009
ISSUE No. 38
- With The Desert Fathers of Egypt: The Coptic Church Today
- Conservation and Restoration at Sinai: Treating a Special Place Gingerly
- In The Valley There Is a Garden: The Spiritual and Cultural Treasury of St. Catherine's Monastery
- Ascent of Mount Sinai

SPRING 2009
ISSUE No. 37
- In Memoriam: Alexander Solzhenitsyn
  I. A Bright Flame   II. The Homecoming   III. The Turn of The Wheel
- The Orthodox Church and Society (Part II): Church-State Relations in Contemporary Russia
- The Living Relic

WINTER 2009
ISSUE No. 36
- To Be Free or Not To Be: Welsh Christianity at The Crossroads
- Safely Home to Heaven
- Melangell with a Thousand Angels
- Hare at Pennant
- The Bright Field: Three Welsh Poems
- The Orthodox Church and Society (Part 1)

FALL 2008
ISSUE No. 35
- Uusi Valamo: Finland's Northern Light
- A Short History of Finnish Orthodoxy
- Jaakko's Finland: A Village Boyhood and Beyond
- Christmas Eve: A Poem by Aleksis Kivi
- The Manifold Nature of Love The Monastery: Mr. Vig and The Nun

SUMMER 2008
ISSUE No. 34
- Greece's Dostoevsky: The Stories of Alexandros Papadiamandis
- A Village Easter: Memories of Childhood
- Mature Fruit and Bright Faith: Spiritual Direction in Contemporary Orthodoxy
- The Hidden Pearl: Rome's Catacombs and The Earliest-Known Image of The Mother of God

SPRING 2008
ISSUE No. 33
- The Life and Times of Fr. David Kirk
- Boyhood in the Deep South
- The Road to Emmaus Runs Through Harlem
- The Archbishop in Alabama

WINTER 2008
ISSUE No. 32
- The Crypto-Christians of Pontus (Part II)
- Banished Faith: The Exile of Christian Pontus
- Return To Kromni
- Between Earth and Heaven: The Monastery of Panagia Soumela
- Yuri Gagarin's Flight To The Heavens: Russia's Believing Cosmonauts

FALL 2007
ISSUE No. 31
- Faith Unseen: The Crypto-Christians of Pontus
- Confessors or Apostates?
- The Dilemma of Crypto-Christianity
- Dialogue of Civilizations: Human Rights, Moral Values, and Cultural Diversity
- The Bath House

SUMMER 2007
ISSUE No. 30

- Bede's World: Early Christianity in the British Isles
- Caedmon's Song
- Orthodoxy in Southern Italy: My Calabria
- The Land That Gave Birth to Saints
- The Children of Magna Graecia

SPRING 2007
ISSUE No. 29

- The Alaskan Orthodox Literary Resurrection
- The Angels of Akun
- Northern Climes: Father John Veniaminov's Akun Diary
- The Orthodox Worldview and C.S. Lewis (Part II)
- Notes On The Jesus Prayer

WINTER 2007
ISSUE No. 28

- The Orthodox Worldview and C. S. Lewis (Part I)
- Celtomania In Eastern Siberia
- Blessed Matrona of Moscow: Saint and Wonderworker
- Answered Prayers at St. Matrona's

FALL 2006
ISSUE No. 27

- Songs of Freedom:
- A Rastafari Road to Orthodoxy
- Nativity Address by Haile Selassie I, Emperor of Ethiopia
- 31st and Troost: From Dividing Line to Gathering Place
- Christmas in the Camp

SUMMER 2006
ISSUE No. 26

- Life on The Golden Horn: Memories of Greek Constantinople, 1948 to 1963
- Hymns and Laments on the Fall of Constantinople
- Interfaith Dialogue: An Orthodox Witness
- The Apples of Transfiguration

SPRING 2006
ISSUE No. 25

- A City of Saints:
- The Forgotten Reliquaries of Paris
- Holy France: The Pilgrim's Road
- Perspective and Grace: Painting The Likeness of Christ
- "Can These Bones Live?"

WINTER 2006
ISSUE No. 24

- Souls In Motion: The Spiritual Life of Teenagers
- Double Faith, Dostoyesvsky and Bulgakov
- Children Behind Bars: A Voice for Greece's Juvenile Offenders
- Anton Chekov: "The Student"
- The Looking Glass: Perpectives on The Teenage Years

FALL 2005
ISSUE No. 23

- Everything In Love: The Making Of A Missionary
- The Pearl of Great Price: Resurrecting Orthodoxy in China
- "I Was Born In An Orthodox World…" – Early Memories of a Chinese Christian
- The Nativity Sermon of St. John Chrysostom

SUMMER 2005
ISSUE No. 22

- Antioch's Golden Hoard: The Chalcedonian Orthodox Manuscript Treasury
- Saints and Scholars of Christian Antioch
- Pillars to Heaven: Stylite Sites of the Levant
- The Village Church of Yegorievka: Part II

SPRING 2005
ISSUE No. 21

- From Jainism to Orthodoxy: An Indian Passage
- Witness For An Apostle: Evidence of St. Thomas in India
- The Indian Verses of St. Ephrem the Syrian
- The Village Church of Yegorievka: Part I

WINTER 2005
ISSUE No. 20
- Eternal Questions: On Heaven and Hell
- The Pearl
- Christ, The Medicine of Life: The Syriac Fathers On The Lord's Descent Into Hell
- St. Milos and The Pascha Egg

FALL 2004
ISSUE No. 19
- The Astonishing Missionary Journeys of The Apostle Andrew
- St. Andrew and The Miraculous Isle of Valaam
- Old Valaam: St. Andrew's Legacy,
- A Contemporary Photomontage
- Heaven, A Cave: Christmas in Bethlehem

SUMMER 2004
ISSUE No. 18
- We Are Going to Live in Paradise: Orthodoxy in the Congo
- Letters From An Apostle: The Inner World of Fr. Cosmas of Zaire
- The Last Priest of Caesarea
- Ascension

SPRING 2004
ISSUE No. 17
- The Golden Thread of Faith: Mental Illness and the Soul
- George, Nadezhda, Tatiana, Sergei, and Michael
- Columba Goes East
- Cadam in Ryazan

WINTER 2004
ISSUE No. 16
- Daughter of Eagles
- Albanian Diary: Ten Days in Shqiperia
- Strength in Numbers
- Orthodox Roots, Bektashi Neighbors

FALL 2003
ISSUE No. 15
- Brittany's Celtic Past
- Tro Breizh: A Pilgrimage to the Seven Saints of Brittany
- Corsican Root and Branch
- Global Perceptions and Local Relations: Pitfalls in Christian-Muslim Dialogue

SUMMER 2003
ISSUE No. 14
- Diveyevo: A Pilgrim's Chronicle
- An Album of Old Sarov and Diveyevo
- 1991: The Return of St. Seraphim's Relics to Diveyevo
- St. Seraphim's Canonization and the Russian Royal Family at Sarov

SPRING 2003
ISSUE No. 13
- Beyond the Great Wall: Orthodoxy In China
- The Lotus Cross
- The Ikon in the Home
- The Lightness of Being (Orthodox)

WINTER 2003
ISSUE No. 12
- The Bones of Contention
- Forgive Us, Merciful Lord
- Living Theology in Thessalonica
- Father Chariton

FALL 2002
ISSUE No. 11
- To Be and Not To Seem:
- My Mother-in-law, Grand Duchess Olga Alexandrovna
- 1919: A Refugee Christmas
- The Kaaba and Jacob's Pillow
- The Christmas Vigil

SUMMER 2002 ISSUE No. 10
- Embracing Spring: The Christopolous Family Of Ioannina
- Icon Of Great Joy: The Tinos Mother Of God
- Bishop Kallistos Ware On Personhood, The Philokalia, And The Jesus Prayer
- Pilgrimage Morning
- Moscow Pastors On Children, The Church, And Free Will

SPRING 2002 ISSUE No. 9
- The Stone In The Blender: Orthodox Greece And Contemporary Europe, Part II
- Saints Alive! (The Bits the Hagiographers Left Out)
- G.K. Chesterton In Russia
- Is Chesterton Worth Reading?
- Singled Out: A Survey of Orthodox Christians

WINTER 2002 ISSUE No. 8
- The Stone in the Blender: Orthodox Greece and Contemporary Europe, Part I
- The Marvelous History of the Holy Cross
- Together out of Time: Mosaics in Moscow
- A Siberian Grandmother on Confession

FALL 2001 ISSUE No. 7
- St. Nicholas Monastery and the Island of the Winds
- The Obedience of Love: An Interview with Sister Gavrilia
- Letters from a Village Matushka
- Orthodox World View: Questions from Readers

SUMMER 2001 ISSUE No. 6
- Orthodoxy in Indonesia: An Interview with Archimandrite Daniel Bambang Dwi Byantoro
- Orthodox Mission Profile: Archimandrite Daniel Byantoro and the Indonesian Mission
- The Prophet and the Pasha: Saint Cosmas of Aitolia and Ali Pasha, the Lion of Ioannina
- The Age of Wood
- Survey of Orthodox Christians

SPRING 2001 ISSUE No. 5
- My Work with English-Speaking Converts (Part III)
- From Moscow to Lindisfarne: A Pilgrimage to the West
- Contemporary Voices for Celtic Christianity
- Saints Alive! (The Bits the Hagiographers Left Out)

WINTER 2001 ISSUE No. 4
- Petersburg's Street Kids Find a Home
- Ephraim of Nea Makri: A Saint for Troubled Youth
- My Work with English-speaking Converts (Part II)

FALL 2000 ISSUE No. 3
- Russian Pickwickians: Dickens from an Orthodox Vantage
- My Work with English-Speaking Converts
- We are Once Again a People
- Christ Visits a Muzhik

SUMMER 2000 ISSUE No. 2
- Orthodox Missionary Outreach: Foma: A Magazine for Doubters
- Excerpts from Foma: So, Why is Confession Necessary?
- The House Blessing
- What Have I Done?
- The Christian Parthenon and St. Paul

SPRING 2000 ISSUE No. 1
- Fire from Heaven: Holy Saturday at the Lord's Tomb
- Teaching Our Children to Pray: Reflections of a Young Mother
- From America to Russia: The Myrrh-Streaming Icon of Tsar Nicholas II

Made in the USA
Coppell, TX
08 May 2020

24991537R00046